Pathway to Spirit

By

Jo Bradley

Introduction

This book is dedicated to all those loving souls that have walked beside me on my journey, and continue to do so. Without their love, support and devotion, my work with Spirit would not have progressed. It is due in part to them, that I am able to impart all that I have learnt to you, the enquirer.

Introduction

When I look back, before I truly came to understand this gift of physical mediumship, I must open- heartedly admit that I was completely naive, and had no understanding of spirit at all. Yes I knew I was different in the fact that I saw and heard things that others around me did not, and yes objects seemed to move all by themselves, electrical equipment played up, and strange raps could be heard in the close vicinity of where I stood. But I had no understanding this was due to my physicality or that it was in preparation for the journey that lay ahead of me. It was simply normal. Several years later when I asked my mother if she thought I was 'weird' she said, as only a mother could, "No love, you're just built differently to the rest of us". Her words have stayed with me and brought much comfort, and to others I have repeated them to, in order to reassure them that, they like me, are not alone.

Those of you that have read my first book, 'Spirit in the Physical', will know how I was guided to the path of developing physical mediumship, through repeated and well planned synchronicities from those on spirit side, a journey which has intrigued and inspired me ever since. Like all good things it has taken much hard work, devotion, patience and love of spirit in both vibrations to push the boundaries that separate us from our dearly departed, and to successfully re-unite physically to speak and interact with them. The journey has been a difficult one at times with much knowledge being gained, in how best to create the correct vibration for the reunions to occur.

I now offer all that I have learnt in my teachings, contained within this book. It is up to all of you, individually, to accept or reject all or part of what I impart to you. All I ask is that knowledge be gained and shared and that you will always remain truthful to yourself and those that touch your lives.

Self-Awareness

Let me take you back, to a few months before the true development of my physical mediumship began.

I had been going through a period in my life, where I had been feeling very isolated and lost. Life was not good at that time. My relationship with my partner had broken down, and I was going through a state of reflection on my life, and all the choices that I had made. Some, which I was not proud of, and others, that had led to terrible consequences, such as me falling prey to violence. This left me feeling very vulnerable and insecure. I was however, very fortunate to have the love of children, siblings, parents and friends, all of whom never at any time judged me or blamed me, for what they say life had thrown at me.

My friends often used to say that I only ever looked for the good in people, and that's why it always came as a shock when people did hurtful things. Maybe they were right, but I felt people should be offered kindness from the first moment of meeting; after all, isn't trust and respect gained that way?

I had sold my business and discovered that having more time to fill had become a mental burden. I was no longer having to prepare meeting notes, dash to appointments, answer telephone calls, or remember to pay the staff's wages, as well as organize and run a busy home. It was time for me to take a slower pace, take up hobbies, and enjoy my young family. But as my mind emptied of all things connected to a business, I found it starting to be swamped with emotions that I had stored neatly away in a compartment of my mind.

These emotions were fuelled by a lack of understanding and coming to terms with situations that had been thrust upon me, or from bad choices I had made throughout my life. As a child I had spent much time day- dreaming, a cocoon I guess for self-protection, but as an adult the time had finally come for me to truly understand who I was, why I had experienced such pain in my life, and how I could turn all that I had learnt into something positive.

I went through many weeks of self-reflection, self-judgment and self-criticism, breaking down each situation and replaying it over and over in my mind. My conscience started to weigh heavy on my heart as realization surfaced, that not only had I felt pain inflicted upon me, but I too had inflicted pain, sometimes intentionally and at other times unintentionally.

It is said that when we pass over to the higher side of life, the summerlands of spirit as I call it, a re-run of your life is played back to you, and you sit and reflect on all the things that you would have done differently. I felt that what I was experiencing at this time in my life was just something similar to this process, no one was judging me, I was judging myself and my actions. I was beginning to take full responsibility for all that I had done and thought in my life.

It took me a number of months to work through all that I had experienced, and fully comprehend what I had learnt from each situation; fear, anxiety, loneliness, loss, trust, honesty, deceit, love etc and to be able to relate them to living a human existence. How can we feel and empathise with other people's problems, if we have not experienced for ourselves? It's a bit like saying to someone who has just got divorced, "I know how you feel", when you have never been married!

A great deal of my thoughts were also spent sending out prayers to those that I had wronged in any way. I felt great pain and shame, as I replayed certain situations over in my mind. Admittedly a lot of these things were carried out during my childhood and adolescence years; children can be so hurtful, but I could not rest easy until I had completed this process. So the ether was filled with prayers and requests asking for forgiveness, from people that I hadn't seen or heard from in some cases for many years.

I was beginning to cleanse myself; I asked for forgiveness, but I also forgave myself for the things that I had done wrong and I finally accepted that I am spirit living a human existence, and as humans, we make bad choices, inflict pain, feel pain but we also have a great capacity for love, to give love and to feel love. I pledged that I would always take responsibility, no matter how painful, for all future thoughts and actions, and that I would never purposefully inflict pain on another soul. At night my prayers were focused on bringing relief to those less fortunate than myself. I am sure I must have nearly driven my guides to the point of utter despair at times, as my ramblings would go on well into the night. But also I still didn't truly understand what it was that I was experiencing or what my true purpose was. Then one morning it happened; I awoke with clarity of mind and purpose, and so my true journey began ....

Early Psychic Experiences

It is well documented that mediums experience psychic episodes from childhood; I was no exception to this.

At the age of 4, I had the classic imaginary friend, of course she was not imaginary at all. Her name was Jodie and she was a guide who came forward to me in the guise of a child. I had been born with severe hearing difficulties, which eventually led me to having my adenoids removed. There was no such thing as grommets in those days! The deafness had caused me to become quite a withdrawn child, partly because it was thought initially I was just a lazy child, and having a sister 14 months older than myself, she did the speaking for both of us. I might add little has changed over the years!! In later years I developed clairaudience (clear hearing), which is when spirit literally whispers in your ear. I do wonder if the deafness at that young age was in preparation for this sensitivity in some way, I guess I shall never know that. This child guide stayed with me until I was about 6, when eventually she withdrew because of conditioning that started during schooling. However, in the couple of years that she was with me, she was very much my best friend. I was insistent that a place at the table was laid for her; my poor mother even had to serve her a dinner at each mealtime. My mother neither encouraged or discouraged, but being clairvoyant she knew that Jodie was by my side.

I also had a terrible tendency to sleep-walk. We lived in a small terraced
house ; the front door was at the bottom of the stairs at the front of the house, and the kitchen, which was the warmest room in the house, was at the back. One night I apparently came downstairs and let myself out of the front door. It was well after 11pm, and it had been snowing quite heavily. I was dressed in just a long nightie, nothing on my feet. I walked all the way to the village, which must have been a good half-mile. Luckily for me the pubs were just emptying and our neighbour was just leaving to set home; she worked as a barmaid.
She immediately saw me, took hold of my hand, and slowly walked me home, being careful not to wake me. My mother was horrified when she opened the door to see me standing there hand in hand with the neighbour, and soaked through. The only memory I have of that night was sitting in front of the open fire in the kitchen, with a warm blanket wrapped around me, and drinking a mug of hot chocolate. My mother ensured she bolted the door before we went to bed, just to be doubly sure the incident was not repeated. You may be saying to yourself, but what does sleepwalking have to do with psychic experiences? Well I believe that those that have the potential to be used as a channel for trance generally sleep- walk, or rather I should say appears to be sleepwalking. I think it should be renamed trance walking.

As a child I was very emotional, but of course being an empath other people's moods greatly affected me. One of the most painful influences on my life was my birth father; he was a prolific gambler and my mother would have to hide money under the floorboards, so that he wouldn't gamble away the rent and food money. This angered him greatly, to the point of threatening us bodily harm, and we would have the Salvation Army regularly turn up in the middle of the night and take us to a place of safety. I still to this day remember men wearing long black coats bundling us into a car and speeding off to a small dark one bedroom flat, on the top floor of a building that sat on the corner of two streets. It added to my confusion of reality; I knew our father cared little about us, but I sensed what could only be described as demons around him. I literally felt them as monsters as children do, but the demon was his gambling addiction. Eventually my mother divorced him and our life became more tranquil.

When I was in my early twenties, I went to view an old cottage in the village where I grew up. I was married with a young daughter who was only a few months old. My grandmother was at that time elderly but still living in a flat in the village, and so when the cottage came on to the market, I felt compelled to go and view it. On contacting the estate agent, my partner and I arranged a viewing at teatime; it was winter and got dark around 4pm. The estate agent gave us instructions that if we arrived first, we were to go around the back and let ourselves in. We arrived some 20 minutes before the appointment and made our way to the back door. It was very dark with no street lighting. My partner opened the door and stepped inside; I could hear him fumbling for a light switch but not finding it. I stepped into what was the old scullery kitchen behind him and no sooner than I did, I was swept over with a terrifying feeling of dread. I started to panic and as I tried to lift my feet to go back out the way I had come, found I was unable to move my feet, it was like they were super glued to the ground. I was shouting to my partner but he dismissed my feelings, believing it was because of the dark. I started to tremble and feel sick with anguish. I quite literally had to launch my body back through the door, and as I did my feet released themselves and I fell to the ground outside. My partner at this point had found the light switch and was looking at me in amazement, as I lay in a crumpled mess on the ground. I got to my feet and started muttering that something awful had happened in this cottage and I refused to step inside again. I headed back towards the car where I waited for him to join me. The estate agent arrived a few minutes later and my partner continued the viewing alone.

We headed towards my grandmother's flat, and as we walked in, her friend Rose was with her. My grandmother asked how we had got on with the viewing. I was still muttering that something horrid had happened there, and that there was no way I would consider living there. Rose enquired as to what property we had viewed; my gran was trying to be evasive with her, but undeterred she asked again. I gave my Gran a fixed stare as I responded, and said the old cottage in the village. Rose immediately told us that the old lady that had lived there had fallen in the kitchen and was unable to get up, no one noticed she had not been about, and she lay on the floor and died. She was not found for several weeks.

This accounted for my feelings of panic, anxiety and the feeling of not being able to move. I had stepped into the room where she had laid on the floor and died!

The next account I am going to share with you is a very painful and emotional one and caused me so much distress at the time; as you read on, you will fully understand why.

I had moved into a semi-detached house in Chesham with my partner; at this stage we had two young daughters aged three and eighteen months. I was unhappy in my marriage; we had been married when I was only nineteen years old, a baby myself really. Shortly after moving in to our new home, I began to notice that the house was always cold, and the sun, even when shining brightly outside, never seemed to radiate into the rooms through the glass of the windows. Visitors never seemed to stay long; they had a feeling of unease. It had been many years since this house had seen a lick of paint, and believing it just needed brightening up, I began to paint each room. However, as I started to make these changes, strange happenings started to occur.

It started on the stairs. As I was walking down one morning, I felt a hand push me from behind; it was not a gentle touch but a hard shove. I don't know how I kept myself from falling the rest of the way down. As the morning progressed I put the incident out of my mind and carried on with my daily tasks, that was until later in the day, when I had cause to go back upstairs to retrieve something, and on the way back down yet again a hard shove in my back!

When my partner returned home that evening, I explained what had happened during the day. He looked a little bemused to be honest, but to pacify me, he climbed the stairs to the top, waited a moment, then walked back down. No shove in the back for him. I started to put it down to a vivid imagination and possible tiredness with two small children.

That night I went to bed but had a very disturbed night, I felt like I had not slept at all. The following morning, the children woke me early as usual, so I collected them from their bedroom, carrying the younger of the two in my arms. I got half way down the stairs when a hard shove in the small of my back quite literally surprised me and threw me off balance; I slipped down two or three of the stairs, crying out as I did so. I don't know how I managed to find my feet again before falling the rest of the way. My small daughter in my arms was terrified and began crying.

I began to be very wary, bracing myself each time I was on the stairs, particularly if I was holding either of my daughters. The disturbed nights were getting worse and I was starting to get dark rings around my eyes, through lack of sleep. Then one night, I started to hear the voice of a man in my dreams; it was not a pleasant voice, and it was a strong controlling voice. He would tell me nasty things and try to get me to do things, dark things, that no ordinary sane person would ever consider doing. My partner, who was not very understanding at the time, probably due to our relationship not being great, started to get concerned and each time I woke and got out of bed, he would wake too and follow me. The voice in my dreams was trying hard to control me. I made a doctor appointment; my doctor who was of a similar age to me was very kind and understanding, and I trusted him and his judgment. As I entered his surgery that day and sat down, he seemed surprised that visually I looked so tired and withdrawn. He asked me what was going on; I told him I felt I was suffering with a mental illness as I was being plagued by a voice in my dreams. We had a long talk and then he declared that he absolutely knew I was as sane as him, and prescribed me some sleeping tablets in the hope that if I managed to get some quality sleep I would soon start to feel better and the voice should stop. Now I am not one for medications, however knowing that I needed help I decided to try them out. It seemed to make matters worse. The voice became louder and still my sleep was greatly disturbed, however the voice became even more sinister and began to enforce that I should harm my children. I was terrified; my partner each night before we went to bed hid all sharp objects, knives, scissors, anything that could cause serious harm. I went back to the doctor, and this time the doctor looked me squarely in the eye and said, "You don't need me, you need a priest!"

My house was on the top of a hill, and in front of us sitting on the side of the hill was our local church. It was a large building with stunning glass windows and a large graveyard in its grounds. I had never visited the church or the local vicar before as my belief was that of a Spiritualist, however, desperate and not knowing where to turn, I found myself pulling open the large wooden door and sitting on a hard wooden bench before the church altar. I was deep in thought, wondering if I was possessed by the devil; it was the only answer left to me. The silence was broken by the voice of a kind and gentle soul who had approached me and sat quietly next to me. I had not been aware of his presence until he spoke. This kindly soul said, "You are troubled my child".

I looked up and placed my gaze upon a young man wearing a white collar; he was smiling at me in a gentle and understanding way. I sat with him and spoke at length about the problems within my home and the voice in my dreams.

I told him I was so very worried that I would harm my children whom I loved dearly. This gentle soul in an unobtrusive way explored things that were a problem in my life, things that I was failing to deal with and choosing to ignore. My marriage was the focus of discussion. I understood that day, when I left him sitting in church, that I was drifting along in life like a piece of drift wood in the open sea. I was not dealing with life's issues or taking responsibility for my own happiness. I was allowing others to control my life and me. But I knew that this kindly soul was not only speaking of those on this side of life controlling me, but also unseen forces, meaning those that reside on the spiritual side of life. "Take back control", he said to me.

I left the church and went home. Clarity of mind was returning to me. When my partner returned from work, I explained that our marriage was causing us harm; it was not fulfilling, it was becoming a burden and causing unhappiness. A wise guide once said to me, many years after this event, that relationships are broken for a reason; he was right. My partner packed a bag and left our home. The very moment the door closed warmth swept through the house and relief swept over me. I did not have any more dreams, the shoving in the back stopped immediately too. I had dealt with the true problem in my life and taken back control; in that moment I had regained my spiritual strength.

A few days later, I went to speak to the kindly vicar at the church, to thank him and reassure him that all was well. As I entered the church I was greeted by an older gentleman; I asked to speak to the young vicar. He explained he was the vicar of the church and had been for many years, but then he paused and said, "You are not the first young lady to have spoken to this man you describe, although I have never set eyes upon him myself". So my kindly soul appeared to be a guiding angel sent to me at my hour of need.

As for the house I was living in, I moved shortly afterwards, but I did make enquiries to see if any previous occupiers had reported any strange occurrences. Apparently a young man had lived there alone before me. He was a businessman but became a recluse, and he was taken from the house not by his own free will. When he was removed he was screaming about the voice that was telling him things; no one knew what became of him. So, I believe my experience with this entity, for surely that's what I believed it to be, showed that it prayed on the vulnerable, as I was at the time, but with a little help from those on spirit side, good prevailed over evil!!

A Fruitless Search

In my first book written by Norman Hutt 'Spirit in the Physical', I shared with you how spirit, through a series of synchronicities, led me to the College of Psychic Studies, based in South Kensington, London, where I studied under the guidance of Tony Stockwell, who in my opinion is one of today's finest mediums, delivering first class survival evidence. It was Tony who highlighted my gift for physical mediumship.

Each week we would start our class with Tony with a guided meditation, and it was during this process that transfiguration first revealed itself. I of course was not aware of the occurrence at the time as I was deep in meditation, but I do remember Tony remarking that I had completely 'gone', not that I knew what he meant at that time with the remark. Transfiguration was still to reveal itself to me.

When I was first told that I possessed the gift of physical mediumship, several questions filled my mind. The first being 'what is it?' and the second 'is this true?' I searched the Internet for what little information I could find, mostly biographies of other mediums that had gone before me. I was disappointed at the lack of information available through such a vast online library, certainly nothing on the development of it, only the end results. I made a decision to source books to further my understanding and then experiment to see what, if anything, would occur, with no expectations other than to learn from whatever was presented to me.

I visited all my local libraries but alas no development book could be found, only books that recounted the evidence from Victorian times mostly. I read all I could of materialization mediums, Helen Duncan, Minnie Harrison and Alec Harris to name just a few. I accessed the website of direct voice medium Leslie Flint, listening intently to the recordings of the dearly departed that had spoken through his mediumship; I was quite frankly amazed and spell bound.
I was fascinated by Daniel Dunglas Home, who had been noted as the king of mediums. Levitation, direct writing, direct voice and materializing spirit hands, were among the phenomena that sitters regularly reported. I was starting to understand the difference between each phenomena that can be produced, but not how it could be produced and what conditions were needed.

I was thirsty for information; I sought assistance from my local spiritualist church, but sadly was told they didn't have my 'sort' amongst them. My 'sort' what did that mean? It wasn't the reaction I was expecting, although to be fair, I don't really know what reaction I was expecting!

I thought I had found the help one day that I so badly needed, when I stumbled quite by chance onto a link to a society dedicated to developing physical mediumship. It was called the Noah's Ark Society. I excitedly sent them correspondence and requested membership. A few days later I received a letter telling me the society was closing, and therefore they could offer me no assistance whatsoever. I was badly disappointed.

A few weeks later, a friend told me of Jenny's sanctuary; she had stumbled upon their website. We decided we would take a drive to Banbury where it was based, which was about an hour's drive. When we arrived a very nice elderly gentleman greeted us, by the name of Ron Gilkes. He explained the centre had been set up in memory of his beloved daughter 'Jenny' who had taken her own life. He happily showed us around the purpose-built building and asked what our interest in physical mediumship was. We chatted and I explained what had taken place on my spiritual journey to date. He was keen for me to become a developing physical medium for the centre and to eventually publicly demonstrate there too.
I said I would give it some thought; he had informed me that I would be expected to attend twice a week every week and that he would provide the sitters. I would have no choice about who he chose. My friend and I spoke about it at length on the journey home.

I came to the conclusion that making that substantial journey twice a week every week was not practical. My children were still young and I also worked full time for my living which involved shift work. Also I was unhappy at not being able to have an input with sitters. I contacted Ron the following day and declined his kind offer; he was disappointed but understood my reasons.
I reflected on what I had managed to establish as facts regarding the

development of physical mediumship, which was, that small groups of people, usually families would gather in a darkened room. The medium would sit inside a cabinet, they called a 'spirit cabinet'. Long metal trumpets with luminous tabs were placed in the room. Trance was often used as a form of communication. That was it, the full extent of my knowledge and not knowing where to search next, I decided to put my faith in spirit, it was time to experiment!

Experimenting with Table Tilting

I was at the point that I really needed to start understanding and exploring the cause behind all the phenomena that I had naturally accepted throughout my life.
Now that Tony had labeled it with a tangible name, I was determined to find out answers that were consuming my mind. But where should I start? At the beginning you would think, but what was the beginning?

We had taken part in an activity called table tilting at College one afternoon, something that Tony had regularly participated in. Table tilting was very popular in the Victorian era, where it was initially treated as a parlour game. However, it quickly became more known for establishing a reliable form of communication with those that had departed this world. Spirit would use the table to tap out letters of the alphabet to spell messages to those present. I remember placing my fingertips on the tabletop along with other students at the College, under the careful instruction from Tony. I was mesmerised when this large wooden dining table started to shudder, then slowly at first it began to glide across the floor of the lecture hall. Students began to squeal with delight, but I was more interested to know, if indeed it was spirit moving the table, how they were moving it?

The table began to move faster and faster as the excitement and noise level of laughter increased in the room. Tony was encouraging all the while, asking for the table to be taken in one direction, then another. Whoever or whatever was in control of this table seemed to have intelligence behind it. I cannot say I was wholly convinced that it wasn't our minds playing tricks on us, or maybe some kind of mind over matter. Maybe it was subconscious reactions, pressure on the table created by our minds' desires for it to respond.

I questioned Tony at the end of the class that day, asking him how it is possible for spirit to be able to move such a large object? He said that spirit are able to utilize our energy, and in some cases by the use of a substance called 'ectoplasm'. I was about to question him further on 'ectoplasm' when the class had to vacate the room. I would save that question till the following week! I decided that once I returned home that evening, I would call a good friend and ask her to participate in experimenting further with table tilting.

My friend arrived at about 9pm, and we meditated for 30 minutes or so. Afterwards, I told her all about the heavy dining table at College and the table tilting experiment. She looked a little incredulous to be honest, but nevertheless agreed we should try.

We settled either side of a coffee table and placed our fingertips upon it. We waited patiently for several minutes but alas it did not move. Undeterred we continued to sit and I remarked that they seemed to respond to laughter. My friend, grinning, made a sound to resemble a laugh, which in turn actually made me laugh. A very loud knock was heard on the centre of the table moments before it shot off in one direction, making us jump to our feet to chase it. Laughter, was this a key element of phenomena?

The table continued to move about the room and seemed to respond to our requests for change of direction. I asked if they could tap once again for us and a quick succession of taps were clearly heard. I asked them to copy what I did, tapping a random amount of times on the tabletop, and each time they tapped back to match the amount I had requested. Indeed there seemed to be intelligence behind the phenomena.

A group of students including myself, started to meet up outside of College. We often met in one of our homes in Kingston, and would read photographs for each other. One evening we decided to do table tilting. The table was a large heavy oak round one with glass laid on the top. It could not be moved by pushing and took several people to physically lift it. We placed our fingertips on the top and started to encourage movement. The evenings always produced much laughter and this particular evening was no different. After a few minutes the table slowly started to move. We continued to encourage and the table moved faster and faster. Raps were heard all over the table. The table started to levitate; it was hovering just above the floor. This proved to me that it could not have been something that we were creating with our own minds. We had not asked the table to lift and yet it did. Our hands were all placed on the tabletop, and yet the table was lifting completely, eliminating any other cause other than something paranormal creating the phenomena.

We then drew up chairs and sat around the table to hold a séance, none of us with a great deal of experience, but we had enthusiasm and a willingness to learn. When I look back I think it was more for my benefit, as they were all aware of what Tony had told me, but knew that I was unsure of what lay ahead and how to proceed. In all honesty I cannot with absolute clarity remember much of this séance, other than the physical feelings that swept over me.

I remember feeling at a great distance from the proceedings, the back of my neck felt like I had tremendous pressure on it pushing me forward. My limbs felt heavy and I remember gasping for breath. The next moment I was fully aware of was when my friends were asking if I was all right? I said I was, but I was confused. They were very excited and said they thought I was going into some sort of trance. Trance? Why? How? One of them stated that they had seen a whitish substance just starting to emanate from my mouth, which they believed to be ectoplasm. What was this ectoplasm? I was about to find out!

Experimenting with Ectoplasm

When I started to experiment with this physical mediumship, I had forgotten that spirit would experiment with me too. They knew that they had my attention and that I was excited and intrigued. I was embracing, but questioning, all that was brought to me, or maybe the correct term would be through me, my physicality, my energy, my whole being.

I was now presented with this ectoplasm. But what is it? A substance? A visible energy? The Oxford dictionary states: a supernatural viscous substance that supposedly exudes from the body of a medium during a spiritualistic trance and forms the material for the manifestation of spirits. I had read many biographies of mediums that worked with this substance, and was aware that it could be potentially harmful. Mediums had been physically hurt, sometimes fatally. The book written by Helen Duncan's daughter, Gena, highlighted the need to be extremely cautious. It seemed that mediums were vulnerable due to the actions of sitters. It is stated that ectoplasm, if exposed to sudden light or touched without warning, retracts back into the medium with great force, which can cause severe burning, internal injuries, and even result in death.
Undeterred, but mindful that I could possibly be dealing with something potentially dangerous, I continued forward to establish the facts.

Although I believed my fellow students account of what had happened during my 'apparent trance', I had not witnessed this substance for myself. It left me still pondering on the question.

One night I awoke in the early hours, and my bedroom was filled with moonlight. As I opened my eyes I was aware that I was laying on my back; this was unusual because I always sleep on my stomach. My eyes took a few seconds to adjust to the brightness of the moonlight, but as they did, I saw a long whitish grey cylindrical shape protruding from my mouth. I was bewildered as to what it could be, and as I was studying it, it started to withdraw back into my mouth. I was unable to move, possibly due to being unsure of what was occurring, but I can say, strangely not through fear. After the object had completely disappeared from my vision, I sat upright in bed. My initial thought was of being unharmed, although I did have an aching in my solar plexus.

When I arrived at College for my next class with Tony, I was still suffering with the ache and kept rubbing the area with my hand, to try to alleviate the discomfort. No words exchanged between my tutor and me, other than him informing me I had an injury due to the extraction of ectoplasm, and that I must proceed with caution. So, this substance had been ectoplasm, and more to the point, I had seen it.

I had for several months been suffering with very disturbed nights. I was being plagued with the most awful dreams, in which I was choking. I would often wake from my sleep with my fingers in my throat, trying to pull out whatever was causing the obstruction. I now believed the dreams to be connected to this process of the withdrawal of ectoplasm.

My experiments continued. I have already recounted in detail in my previous book 'Spirit in the Physical', the séance which I held with friends in my home, where a black mass appeared from under the table in front of me, and as it started to move across the table, formed a perfectly shaped hand. On another occasion, a pair of feet complete with boots manifested in my living room, whilst I was giving a reading to a lady referred to me by a friend. Both incidents had instilled terror into those present, but these occurrences were filling me with a desire to truly understand the workings of spirit, through this form of mediumship. I was also noticing that when ectoplasm was present in the room, it had a peculiar odor, a very earthy damp smell. Not particularly pleasant to the nose, and the more ectoplasm, the greater intensity of smell!

I was absorbing knowledge as quickly as a sponge soaks up water. I had learnt so far that ectoplasm is drawn from the body, that it can be white, grey or black and that it can be molded into shapes. It has a strong odour, it also could operate at a distance, could cause harm to the physical body, and be seen in varying shades of light.

I have always known that mediumship has a purpose, that being to bring the two realms together, to prove that life continues when we leave this earth plane. The proof offers healing to the bereaved and confirms that love is the key to our continued connection to each other. I needed to know if spirit could utilize ectoplasm, for the purpose of identification of those that have passed from this world. Feet and hands materializing with the use of this substance was amazing, however, we do not identify each other generally by our feet, but by our faces. I didn't have to wait long before I received my answer.

Experimenting with Transfiguration

One Spring evening, a friend called around for a coffee and a chat. We were discussing all things spiritual as we often did. My friend had followed the Mormon faith and I was always interested in hearing of their teachings.

I made some more coffee as she enquired how my investigation into physical mediumship was progressing. I told her all that I had learnt so far, as we settled back on to the sofas in my lounge. I began to feel really uncomfortable; I seemed to be having a hot flush. I opened the lounge window to allow the breeze to come into the room, and my friend asked if I was feeling ok, to which I responded "Yes, other than my rising temperature". We continued to talk, but my discomfort grew.

I was feeling heavy in my body and the hot flush continued. My friend was staring at me rather strangely. I asked her what was wrong; she cocked her head to one side then the other. She rubbed her eyes with her hands; I asked her again what was wrong? She replied, "You look very strange, very strange indeed". I asked in what way? She said my face had changed shape and what looked like a moustache had appeared under my nose, which had enlarged! I managed to get to my feet and took a look at my reflection in the mirror that hung above my fireplace on the lounge wall. I was shocked to see the image of a man looking back at me. I later discovered this man to be Dan, one of my guides.
So this was my introduction to transfiguration.

The following few days brought many questions to my mind. I had previously wondered if ectoplasm could be used for identification purposes of souls. The transfiguration a few nights earlier had answered that question to some degree. I had most certainly, along with my friend, seen the clear image of a man. I had also noted the daylight conditions in the room and again I was unharmed by the process.

The next question I needed to know the answer to was; is it possible for transfiguration to be shown on other people who were not mediums, in a safe but very visual form? The answer came about a week later.

Several friends had come to my home for a social evening. We had scented candles alight in the room and we were all relaxing and enjoying each other's company. The conversation was a happy one with much laughter; of course, laughter being a key ingredient to physical phenomena, the vibrations were being raised in the room. I was not conscious of this fact though as it was simply a social evening. My friend, who had been present when the transfiguration had occurred, was also present on this social evening. She started to tell the group what had happened and what she had witnessed. The group was intrigued by this and asked the normal questions such as, are you sure it was not your imagination? She clearly reminded them of the fact she had little knowledge on the subject, so why would her imagination conjure up such an image, particularly as she was not even clairvoyant herself? We started to debate the subject but could not understand how spirit could project their image using the substance called ectoplasm over the mediums face. I voiced my question to the group regarding the use of ectoplasm, and if it were possible for spirit to produce the same effect on a person without psychic sensitivities. A moment later the friend who was sat closest to me started to fidget in her chair; she said she was feeling rather warm, and the rest of the group started to tease her, saying her imagination was now active. However, as we looked at her, a dark circle formed around her eye as if she was sporting a black eye.

I was mesmerised by this occurrence and was studying it closely, when the friend sat the other side of her also started to fidget and complain of feeling hot too. A moment later, she was also sporting a black eye! One by one each friend experienced the same physical effects and each had a darkened eye. In each case their left eye was affected. This process harmed none of my friends. This was the answer to my question. This form of transfiguration was to feature much more in later years, as you will read later in the book.

As my curiosity grew with these phenomena we decided to dedicate some time to see if the visual effects could be developed by spirit. I started to sit every week for about an hour and give myself over to spirit. It was almost a meditative state of relaxation that I used, and of course there was the intention to progress in this field. Development seemed to occur at an extraordinary pace. One evening a friend of my son called at the house to see him, and it happened to be at a time when we were about to sit for further transfiguration development. He seemed to have a healthy enquiring mind, and having been told by my son that strange things occurred around me, he asked if he could join us for the session. He was over the age of 18, and, satisfied it was through a genuine desire to experience, I was happy to agree. That evening a veil of ectoplasm was clearly seen to pour over my face, before a gentleman with a pointed beard revealed himself using the ectoplasm, to those present. There was stunned silence and looks of astonishment at the end of the sitting.

Spirit was really starting to prove that death was simply just another dimension.

The following evening, my friend arrived for our nightly meditation, she on one sofa and I sat on the other. Meditation was an important part of my connection to spirit. That evening we had been meditating for about twenty minutes when a strange whooshing sound started in the room and it grew in volume. I started to withdraw from meditation when the whooshing noise changed to that of a voice of a woman. She called my friend's name. Believing it was only me that could hear the sound, I did not respond, however, my friend did!

I opened my eyes now fully conscious again to see my friend grinning at me and very excited at this new development. We soon discovered it was a phenomenon called independent direct voice, and so the development took us in yet another direction......

Experimenting with Direct Voice

Direct voice is a rare phenomenon these days. I had stumbled on the website of Leslie Flint, a noted direct voice medium, whilst trying to find information regarding physical mediumship. His website is full of recordings and is absolutely fascinating. The recordings vary in quality, but all the communicators bring messages to prove that they are more alive in the spiritual realms than when they walked the earth plane.

I had never imagined when I had taken time to listen to some of the recordings, that my own mediumship could or would produce this phenomenon. Before going on further I need to explain the difference between direct voice and independent direct voice, independent direct voice being the rarest form.

Direct voice is a voice from someone on spirit side of life, speaking through what is called a spirit trumpet, a long metal cone. The trumpet is generally moved around the room, suspended in mid- air and is used to amplify the voice so that it can be clearly heard. An ectoplasmic voice box is created inside the trumpet and the trumpet is moved by the use of ectoplasmic rods, attached to the medium.

Independent direct voice is a voice from someone on spirit side speaking seemingly from any point, but generally quite close to the medium from a space in mid- air. Leslie Flint demonstrated independent direct voice. However, generally this phenomenon is produced in a room that is completely blacked out of any light source, light of course not being conducive to ectoplasm.

I have already written in the previous chapter of our first introduction to independent direct voice. This was just the beginning of spirit experimenting with this phenomenon. It became quite commonplace for voices of the deceased to be heard, in particular for visitors to my home to hear their loved ones calling their names. Despite what I had read about this phenomenon there seemed to be one thing lacking, that being total darkness. This phenomenon always seemed to take place in some form of lighting, red light, candlelight and daylight, it seemed to make little difference. The only minor difference would be the strength or clarity of the voice.

I had a young man come to my home one day to receive healing, and had a low wattage red bulb alight in the lamp. The poor lad jumped with fright when his name was repeatedly called out, and it only stopped when he acknowledged the voice. I was not aware at the time that spirit are unable to hear their own voice in our vibration so it is only when we acknowledge them that they know they can be heard.

A gentleman visiting from Australia who had lost his wife a few years earlier also had the pleasure of hearing her voice, again in good lit conditions. What I had noticed was it seemed to occur spontaneously and generally when I was feeling relaxed, and either channeling healing or discussing spiritual matters.

The voices at this early stage only ever managed to say a few words, but this was to be further developed. In my previous book 'Spirit in the Physical' I recounted the independent direct voice which took place at my father's bedside during the last hours before he passed. It was that experience which truly taught me the healing properties of mediumship. I don't believe that up until that point I had fully appreciated the true power of spirit communication, and in particular direct communication, meaning spirit voices speaking from the spiritual side of life, directly projected in their own voices into our vibration. It is truly remarkable.

I began to heal before my father passed and I feel strongly that no other experience could have helped me in the same way. I know many of you reading this book will find it hard to believe that a medium, who is clairaudient and clairvoyant, and knows that life continues after the death of our physical bodies, would struggle so much with bereavement.
But the fact was that my father had no belief in an afterlife, he believed that once you're dead, you're dead, black hole, nothing, end of existence. This caused me great concern; I knew he would wake up on the other side free from a diseased body, but I worried that he would reject whoever came for him, believing he was hallucinating. It was him acknowledging his mother calling his name, and my realization that he had finally accepted there was something more awaiting him, that brought relief and peace of mind to me.

Spirit continued practicing independent direct voice, and it was not unusual for it to be heard at night after retiring to bed. On one particular occasion, my mother and my sister were visiting from Somerset for a couple of days. I had by this time two spare bedrooms as my children were all becoming independent and setting up home with partners and friends. My son still remained at home.
We all retired to bed at the same time; my sister had already climbed into bed and was just settling herself. She has always slept with her bedroom door open and it was no different even in my home. My mother was in the bathroom and my son was in his room. I had just climbed into bed, when a very loud groan rattled through the

house. I sat upright and quietly said, "I can hear you, but please stop because my sister will not be amused." The groan again rattled through the house. My son came onto the landing from his room, just as my mother came out of the bathroom, and he said, "Please tell me Nan that was you". My mother, from sheer surprise, responded with, "No love, it's not me". My son, who seemed a little panicked at this stage, grumbled under his breath and returned to his room, and my sister lay shaking under the duvet. My mother ended up spending the night sleeping with my sister; thank goodness the spare room had a double bed!

Experimenting with Physical Healing

I must be honest with you all, I had little understanding or belief in any type of spiritual healing, preferring orthodox medicine when absolutely necessary to see a doctor, which thankfully was not often. My journey began with healing, or rather should I say as a channel for healing, one evening at a friend's house, previously described in 'Spirit in the Physical'.

One evening a friend asked if I would run a meditation circle at her home. I agreed and we gathered at her house. She had replaced the bulb in her living room lamp with a red one. I had no idea why she had done this, but she seemed happy with her preparations. Everyone started to arrive and take their seats. As one lady walked across the room accompanied by her daughter, I noticed she was limping. I enquired as to what was wrong with her leg. She told me she had fallen a couple of weeks earlier, and it was still swollen and difficult to put weight on. For some strange reason I immediately offered to give her some healing. This was strange because, although I have never doubted the power of spirit, I had never actually placed my hands upon anyone before. Her daughter immediately started to say, "Oh, that's daft, all that nonsense", but the lady motioned to her daughter to be quiet, and said, " Yes, I would appreciate you trying".

I threw my thoughts to the guides and asked for a healing to take place, and no sooner had I put my hands upon her knee, this dark hand almost like a hand wearing a black glove appeared over mine. I was shocked to say the least, but completely mesmerised at the same time. This hand seemed to dart through my fingers and inside the lady's knee.

I couldn't have removed my hands at that point, even if I had wanted to, as it seemed they were almost glued to her. I could feel things being moved around under my hand. I glanced at the woman, who was just simply sat staring in complete surprise at what was going on. Her daughter started to stutter, "I can see something, oh my God, what is going on"? All the others in the room had gathered around to watch this event take place. After a few moments the hand seemed to withdraw from her knee and appear over mine once again, and then gone, it vanished as quickly as it had appeared. My hands were released and I sat back on my heels. I looked at the woman and said, "What happened there"? She said nothing, got to her feet and walked minus the limp across the room. Her daughter at this point had stopped stuttering and was completely unable to talk!

The meditation circle did not take place that evening, instead a long and exciting debate took place. It was the first of many wonderful experiences in this area of my work, which is not in any way a replacement for conventional medicine, but does in my opinion greatly assist in the healing process.

A tutor at the College of Psychic Studies in London had once both terrified and intrigued me by stating that I would progress with healing using my physical mediumship abilities. On questioning what she meant by this, she stated that I would be used as a channel for psychic surgery. I raised an eyebrow at her and enquired further as this was something that I had not heard of previously.

She fixed her gaze upon me and ever so confidently said, "You will be used by spirit, so that they can perform operations". EEK!

But how could this be true? I was yet to learn that physical illness is energy, manifesting around an organ or system in the body, and very often is brought about by stress, anxiety or poor choices. I guess my first experience at the meditation circle had been just as she had described.

I received an e-mail from a lady enquiring if her husband, who was suffering from motor neuron disease, could join my physical circle. We were looking for dedicated sitters so that we could start a circle. I wrote back telling her he was more than welcome to come to my home, so that we could talk through his suitability. A couple of weeks later John arrived with his friend Alex, who had to drive John because John had lost the use of both his arms through the illness. They were both lovely men and very spiritual and inquisitive to learn more. They were both welcomed to join our newly formed circle.

However, it was John that allowed me to experiment with the energy channeled for physical healing. He felt it could do him no harm, as there was no cure for the illness he was suffering from, from orthodox medicine.

One evening after circle, John and I were sat in the living room chatting about the evening's events. Alex was in the kitchen with the circle leader making coffee. John remarked that his motor neurons was worsening as his legs had started to feel weak. I suggested that maybe I could try some healing on him, and rubbing my hands together to activate the energy, I rose from the sofa. As I took one step towards him my hands parted, and a bolt of energy shot from the palm of my right hand and struck John on the forehead. His head was thrust backwards and he sat quivering as if receiving an electric shock. He made a strange moaning sound, which lasted several seconds. Through fear I started to laugh uncontrollably, but my mind was in a whirl trying to analysis what was taking place. I thrust my palms back together and immediately shut off the energy, and John's head came back up to the normal position. I nervously observed him as he asked, "What did you do to me"? I had not got a clue what I had done, it was a complete mystery to me.

The energy can only be described as blue, and looked like a bolt of lightning that came from my palm, and connected with his forehead, and that it could be seen with the physical eyes. I knew that psychic people are very prone to static shocks; it is one of the indicators that someone has psychic ability, but this was so much more than a static shock!

John seemed to have no ill effects from the experience and it did not seem to put him off being a guinea pig, in fact quite the reverse; he was adamant that I needed to learn how to work with this energy, and encouraged me at every opportunity to channel it. Although I must admit the experience had frightened me, fear of course comes from lack of knowledge.

I continued for several months with John's encouragement and willingness to be experimented on and eventually began to use this energy with good results. I say 'use' this energy; I should say 'be used' as a channel for this energy by those in spirit working through me. I very quickly established that it truly was a physical energy, an energy that could manifest hands that seemed to dart into the body of those requiring healing, an energy that could be felt by the receiver, but also an energy that could often be accompanied by sound. What do I mean by sound? Well, what I mean is, often the receiver would hear voices calling to them during a healing session, what we term direct voice.

The more I channeled this energy, the stronger the connection became.

I suddenly became aware of seeing inside the body, looking at organs and cells. I am not medically trained in any sense other than being a first aider, so this was quite mesmerising to me. It seemed that whoever controlled this energy through me from spirit side was almost giving me an x- ray vision with it. I would give a commentary to the receiver, of where the energy was being used in their body and why!

One evening while visiting a friend, a gentleman arrived unexpectedly; he was known to my friend, who had known him for many years. She invited him in and introduced us. This man calling at her house on that evening I believe was no coincidence, as he was suffering with a shoulder problem and was unable to raise his arm above his head. I enquired as to what had been the cause, but he had no reply other than he had woken with the problem. I asked if I could place my hands upon him, to which he agreed, but I was surprised when the guide working with me took my x- ray vision to his stomach rather than his shoulder.

As I peered at internal body parts I was shown a stomach ulcer that was well established. I told him what I was being shown and he confirmed that he was indeed suffering with one. Then I was taken to his heart and listened to a heartbeat that was irregular, again he confirmed that he had been born with a heart condition and regularly saw a specialist for check- ups. I became aware that I was actually unable to remove my hands from him; they seemed to be super- glued to him. The gentleman stated that his stomach was feeling extremely hot on the inside and that he could feel movement around his heart. Moments later my hands were released and I removed them from him. We chatted for a few minutes after the healing session and he explained that the stomach ulcer had been with him for a very long time, that he had to avoid certain foods like fried food, and that he often had to take remedial medication to alleviate pain and discomfort.

About a week later there was a knock at my door, and there stood the same man, with a smile on his face; he asked if he could come in for a few minutes. He stated he had been to see his heart specialist that morning, but that it had been a new young doctor running the clinic.
He said the doctor was baffled, as the notes stated there was a heart complaint and he couldn't find any trace of it, during the examination!

So had the healing produced this result? I guess we will never truly know the answer to that. You are probably wondering about the ulcer and the troublesome shoulder? Well, as God is my witness, the gentleman lifted his arm high above his head; he said it had been perfectly fine within an hour of the healing session, and that not one drop of remedial medication had passed his lips for his stomach ulcer either. Maybe the ulcer had gone or maybe it simply did not pain him anymore, either way he was happy and that was all that counted.

A tribute to my friend John

John lived in Kent with his second wife and had six children, three from each marriage. He was a family man at heart; his family was always at the front of his thoughts. John had been a professional footballer in his younger years but became an accountant and businessman after his football career ended.
I can honestly say that the day I met John, my life became richer in every spiritual way possible. He was a kind and gentle soul and despite facing such an awful illness, he was always happy and cheerful. We had a connection that was on a deep soul level, one that cannot be truly put into words to give it full justice. We spent many long hours talking about death, dying and the afterlife. These were subjects that he dearly wanted to speak to his wife about, but she found it too upsetting to confront these issues in light of her husband's pending demise.
John had a very infectious laugh, I fondly nick named him Mutley.
He was highly intelligent and self-motivated, but had the ability to engage people on all levels, whatever their social background. I only had the pleasure of having this special soul in my life for three short years, but he brought so much to me by way of understanding illness and how it affected people and their families when faced with terminal illness.
The world is a much poorer place without him - I miss you my friend.

Other Strange Occurrences

Strange happenings in the shape of physical phenomena were not the only strange happenings that started to occur. On numerous occasions random people would knock on my front door or e-mail me, proclaiming that they had been led to me for various reasons. Never one to ignore people that have taken the time to contact me, whatever their reason for doing so, I replied offering assistance wherever I could, or referring them to local mediums or organizations that I felt could guide them well. Those that came to my front door were shown the same courtesy by way of giving them time to talk and express their needs.

One lady knocked on my door and on me opening it, she said, "You are my teacher"; I found this very curious, as I was simply a student myself.

On another occasion, on opening the door, I found a gentleman who had a goatee beard and who was wearing what looked like workman's clothes; he was holding a carrier bag and had ridden his bicycle to my home. He said, "Hello", and then said, "Ah, you look just as I was shown". I was quite frankly mystified and invited him in for a coffee and a chat. He opened his bag and pulled out two beautiful handmade candles that he had actually made himself. "These are for you," he said. This gentleman explained that he had been living in a Scottish village amongst a group of spiritual people and they had what he referred to as a community.

This community offered spiritual guidance and healing in exchange for small donations for anyone in need of their services. He had been living there with his wife and children for a couple of years and was a channel for healing, but he was suffering from carpal tunnel syndrome, and due to the numbness was unable to continue, which saddened him greatly.

One evening while meditating, he asked for help from spirit side, and he claimed to have been given a vision of the healer who could help him resolve his problem.

I was more than sceptical to be honest, however, he was a gentle kind soul, so I agreed to try to help him. I worked on each hand and wrist separately whilst he chatted about his life in Scotland. The following day he telephoned me to say he was pain free, the numbness had gone, and that he was heading back to his beloved community. Had the healing helped? Well, I really don't know, but as far as I am aware he did return and has remained there ever since.

I was becoming very interested in all forms of healing from crystals, colour therapy, reiki, and trance healing. The College of Psychic Studies had a one-day workshop on trance healing advertised in their programme, and the tutor just happened to be my tutor Tony, so I booked a place.

Tony seemed to be quite excited that I was attending as he was keen to witness psychic surgery, however I arrived an hour late for the workshop as the trains had been delayed at Baker Street. When I eventually arrived I was feeling flustered, but Tony in his usual calm manner gave me a few minutes to settle myself. I was amongst students that I had not previously met, so Tony introduced me to the rest of the group; there were about twenty students in all. He briefly explained that I was a developing physical medium and that psychic surgery had just started to manifest. However, he was quick to point out that the college had given him strict instructions that no psychic surgery could be performed due to insurance coverage. It was disappointing as there was students present that I feel could have benefited greatly, however, I learnt a lot that day. I have always found Tony to be an excellent tutor in whatever area he is focused on.

I was seated next to a gentleman at the workshop. He was a beginner and was trying to experience as much as he could to help him with his own spiritual gifts. He was working within a Spiritualist Church delivering clairvoyance as a fledgling whenever the opportunity arose for him. He, unfortunately that day, was to learn the hard way regarding the right to privacy. Tony had asked us to pair up and then gave us an exercise to do, however this man for whatever reason had decided he would give me a clairvoyant reading instead. He started to give me what he thought was evidence from spirit and was rather surprised when I raised my hand and told him to stop. He asked what the problem was, and I told him in no uncertain terms that he was the problem!

It is very easy as a clairvoyant to get carried away, we assume that everyone wants a reading, but that is simply not true. I always make a point of not intruding into people's lives unless they invite me to do so. My friends always assume that they don't have to tell me anything because I will know anyway, but we live in a physical world where our movements are constantly monitored in one form or another and so the right to privacy is important to me, and probably to all of you too, and besides with friends I want them to share with me aspects of their lives, their feelings, their worries, their aspirations as they choose to share with me, because they want to because I'm their friend. I do not use my connection with spirit simply to be nosy or to gain insights that others might not wish to confide in me, I would consider it rude!

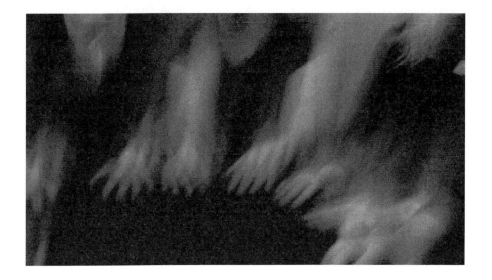

Experimenting with Spirit Lights

I was experiencing some very wonderful phenomena and I have to say that the spirit lights that were displayed to me and visitors to my home would come into this category as well. Being clairvoyant it was not unusual for me to see twinkly fairy lights in differing colours, but it was very unusual for others around me to see them as well, which was happening more and more.

Christmas was approaching and the weather had grown cold with frosty mornings and icy nights. My ex- sister-in- law had popped over for a coffee and brought with her a large tin of sweets by way of a Christmas gift. Both of us were living busy lives, we rarely saw each other, so took the opportunity to have a good chat exchanging all our news concerning family matters.
We were happily chatting when my visitor suddenly pointed her finger in the direction of my Victorian fireplace. "Good God", she said, "What are they"? As I looked in the direction of her pointing finger I saw large balls of light, all different colours, darting in and out of the fireplace. Thinking there must be something wrong with my eyes, I asked her to confirm what she saw. "Well big balls of coloured lights", she replied, "look at them, what are they? And where are they coming from?", she asked. We sat watching them absolutely mesmerised for some five minutes before they shot up the chimney and out of sight. The colours had been so vibrant, similar to those contained in the auric field, for anyone who has ever had the pleasure of seeing them.

On another occasion, a friend who was the editor of a well-known psychic publication was visiting. We were relaxing when a ball of white light appeared close to the floor in front of us. We searched for an ordinary explanation but found no light source which could of accounted for it. The light also kept dimming out then brightening up repeatedly as if being operated by a dimmer switch. Again it stayed for a few minutes before fading out completely.

As you will read further in the book, these balls of light were to play an important role in our circles development, but at this early stage spirit were practicing at every opportunity and ensuring that they were truly producing objective evidence. I guess thinking back there would have been little point in just bringing this wonderful phenomena to me to witness, as I am clairvoyant and therefore would have put my experiences down to clairvoyance, rather than physical phenomena. The phenomena had to be witnessed and acknowledged by those that did not possess the same gift. Spirit needed to be sure that all could see or hear.

Experimenting with Trance

Well, what can be said about trance? Other than it is the most peculiar state of consciousness that can be experienced!
I say this not to be amusing but simply to be truthful.

My first experience of witnessing this form of communication was at the college when my tutor Tony demonstrated it with his guide 'Star'. I was intrigued, having never before sat with such a wise and loving soul speaking through an instrument on this physical plane. I was like a sponge absorbing all I could from this fascinating display of oneness.
The second opportunity came when I booked to see a young medium, to have a trance reading. His name was Jay Love and again he was, at that time, based at the College of Psychic Studies. His guide 'Jafar' is a loving soul, who spoke through Jay with such tenderness towards me, and brought forward many details of the work with spirit that lay ahead of me regarding mental and physical mediumship. The full details of that sitting are in my previous book, so I will not transcribe it here again, but I can say with honesty that all that was foretold during that sitting has indeed come to pass.

It was shortly after this sitting with Jay that I started to notice a change, maybe even what one would class as a shift within me. It started to occur during meditation. I noticed that I was becoming less and less aware of the physical vibration around me, and a deeper connection to my higher self was revealing itself. This was wonderful, that is until an overwhelming feeling of nausea and needing to vomit swept over me each time I attempted to meditate, and I would have to rush myself back to full consciousness. The first few times it happened I tried to convince myself that it was simply mind over matter, almost a feeling I had conjured up myself, for what purpose though I had no idea. However, this feeling of nausea continued for several weeks. I was very emotional during this time, crying at the slightest thing or becoming engulfed with rage at small annoyances. The thought that this could be connected to trance mediumship had not entered my head, why would it?

I have since learnt that during the early stages of trance development, we the instruments become highly emotional and sensitive to everything, and I do mean everything. Food, weather conditions, even taste buds are affected.

I had already experienced what my friends had termed as some sort of trance during the table tilting session with my friends from College, where a white substance was seen to start emanating from my mouth, but trance was to reveal itself further.

My daughter aged just 14 and a friend were both used as channels to bring messages directly from the guides to me. Like transfiguration this sensitivity could be transferred to a third person providing there was the presence of a physical medium. Both accounts are in 'Spirit in the Physical'. Interestingly, both my daughter and I were chronic sleepwalkers as small children; perhaps this is a training ground for future psychic development in the area of trance. My daughter has not been used in this way since, but she is a young woman now and has no interest in developing any gifts that she has currently; maybe it is something for her future.

Light trance states, or overshadowing as it should be correctly termed, manifested in other ways too. Often when talking on my computer to friends or acquaintances, particularly during spiritual debates, I would feel very drifty in my consciousness and heavy in my body, my face would tingle and my thoughts felt as though they were not my thoughts but belonged to someone else. Inspirational some would say, and perhaps that would be a true assessment of the words that would come to me. I would see at times whole sentences appearing before me on the screen but when I read them back it was as if I was reading them for the first time. Someone else had put them there, my fingers had not typed them, but no one else's fingers had touched the keyboard. It was the same when I would be chatting with family or friends, often words or sentences would come from my mouth, but they were not my words or even my thoughts of words to speak, they just popped out from nowhere, and would be greeted at times with laughter and at other times with annoyance. I was teased a lot by friends, the normal retort being, "Just be yourself", to which I would reply, "Tonight, I'm going to be" !

I have to admit to you, that of all the experimenting into the different phenomena that was taking place during this time, the overshadowing or light trance state was my least favourite. I say this for two reasons. Firstly, I had experimented and heard on numerous occasions independent direct voice. It seemed to be a good means of communication from those on spirit side; I considered it to be 'pure', meaning there was no interference with the words spoken directly from them, whereas all other forms of communication seemed to be dependent on the ability of the medium it was being channeled through. Secondly, the physical feelings on the body and the mind when over shadowing or a light trance state is being used are uncomfortable and confusing.

I didn't understand the purpose, I suppose, of trance at that early stage of my development. If independent direct voice was achieved with good results, why was there a need for trance? With everything spiritual, all has a purpose, but it could be many months or even years before that true purpose is revealed. Armed with all that I had learnt, it was time to step up development and create a safe place where the true development with spirit could begin....

The Circle of Friends; the Early Days

All that you read here is taken directly from the circle record books. You would think that with all the evidence I had already been given, that development would take only a few months. This was not the case at all; it is a long and winding path and requires an abundance of patience, dedication, an ability to assess conditions created by us, and a willingness to change or adapt those conditions when faced with situations that have a negative impact on the development of the circle.

The creation of the circle

I had placed an advert for suitable sitters and had several responses. I believed I chose the sitters well, based on their intentions for wanting to join. The circle was made up of seven of us, Terry, Julie, Mike, Jayne, Alex, John and me.
Terry is my ex- partner, but we have a very close relationship of friendship still, and have complete trust in each other. Julie and Mike were neighbors and friends of ours. Jayne was a friend who I met through our local Spiritualist Church and who was developing her own mediumistic gifts. John and Alex were both from Kent, and had been best friends for many years. They were lovely gentlemen, both very open to any possibilities of a spiritual nature. John unfortunately was suffering with motor neuron disease and was therefore very drawn to psychic surgery, for which on occasions I was used as a channel by spirit. We agreed the sittings should take place on Friday evenings.

The sittings were to take place in my lounge with doors and windows blacked out by curtains. A cabinet was constructed of old poles and black material, and a dining chair placed inside for me to sit on. Taped music was to be used to lift the vibrations, and a table with luminous paint to provide a little light and focus, because sitting in dark conditions can be a little disorientating. One sitter, Mike, was given permission to use his digital camera in circle. It must be noted that I do not endorse dark séances, but back in 2005 I was conditioned by those on the physical plane on how one should conduct a physical séance, and did not have at that time the wisdom of our spiritual teachers.

First sitting 7th January 2005

None of the members had any previous experience of a physical circle with the exception of me, as I had attended a four-week course at the College of Psychic Studies in November 2004. We sat in the pitch black and were told this was the way to develop physical mediumship.
I entered the cabinet and took my seat on the chair inside; the other sitters formed a circle using the sofas. Julie, who was circle leader at that time, opened with a prayer and we began to sing to raise the vibrations. The table with the luminous paint on it, which had been placed outside of the cabinet, rose two to three feet off the ground and stayed there the entire sitting. I could hear great excitement in the room. Mike, who had the camera, started to take random photographs around the room. I kept asking for updates from the sitters, then I became aware of what I can only describe as a swirling sensation around me; it started at my feet, and the air was icy cold. The sitters reported seeing a white mass float from the cabinet and Mike took a photograph of it. The table floated back down to the ground and the energy in the

room dropped, so the circle was brought to a close with a short prayer and thanks.

The photographs were uploaded onto the computer, and everyone was amazed to see the white mass actually appeared to be the figure of a man complete with pointed beard floating on his side, and the face of a woman. Mike, who had taken the photograph, immediately claimed ownership of the photograph; it became a battle between some of the sitters, and a few days later Mike declared copyright of it. I was devastated and feeling rather hurt at all the upset.

Then the circle guides decided to assist. Over a period of two days, which were the 18th and 19th January, twenty-one apported notes arrived, just dropping from the ceiling. The full account is in 'Spirit in the Physical'. Two of the notes spoke directly about the photographs and stated that Mike was being disrespectful. They asked for him to be removed from the circle. I have always followed the requests from the guides, so I asked Mike to step out, which he duly did.

It took a few years before he knocked on my door, very apologetic, and simply said he had been so overwhelmed by what had taken place at that first sitting and the photographic evidence, he had clearly got caught up in the sensationalism of it all. He was remorseful with how badly he had behaved. I accepted his apology, but have not extended any further invitations to the circle.

Jayne also decided to leave; she wanted to further her own development with her mediumship, and preferred to concentrate on the angelic realms, so she left a few weeks later. Thinking back, I don't think she really knew what a physical circle was, but as I was to find out, sitting in a physical circle is not suited to everyone, and not everyone is suitable to sit despite them believing they are. With losing two circle members so soon after the circle had formed, we decided we would advertise for another sitter, a female. We placed an advert on a website and within days had a lady contact us; I will call her Sarah to protect her identity. We agreed to meet her and have a chat. She was living in London and was recently bereaved, hence why her search for evidence of an afterlife had begun. We agreed for her to join on a trial basis, just to make sure the other members of the circle liked her, and to assess her suitability.

On the day of the sitting Sarah arrived in good time and introduced herself to the other members. She was very keen and participated in singing and chatting and seemed to blend well with everyone present. However, what I did not fully appreciate was the mindset of the bereaved. What do I mean by this?

Bereavement is something that unfortunately we all experience at some time in our lives. There are five stages of loss and grief, denial and isolation, anger, bargaining, depression and finally acceptance.

I should have identified as the weeks passed that Sarah's grief was still unbearable to her, but I am ashamed to say, that I didn't.

That was until I started to notice that during each sitting when phenomena occurred, that she would automatically attribute it to being her partner trying to come through. I tried to push my thoughts to the back of my mind to be kind I suppose. Having suffered bereavement myself I understand the pain and the longing of having just one more chance of seeing or speaking to a loved one on the other side.

Meanwhile, Julie left the circle as she started a relationship with Mike. Given the reason for Mike's departure, she didn't want anything to disturb the development or the harmony of the circle, so she chose to leave.
John was becoming sicker with his motor neurons as well and at times would miss circle because he was too ill to attend, which meant Alex would not attend either.
The circle members were dwindling, which could be another reason why I was so blind to Sarah's neediness as a bereaved person. I say neediness purely as an observation, not through malice. We are all very needy when we suffer loss. I was later to understand, that this was all part of the learning, especially when I began to tutor other circles and groups, but at the time when you are struggling to get the energies right in your circle, it becomes very frustrating and disheartening.

The weeks continued to pass and the development in circle was going in waves. One week would be fairly active and then followed by several sittings where nothing seemed to occur. It took me a long time to understand that not every sitting will be outwardly exciting. In fact the most development is taking place when nothing seemingly occurs. We can only produce a certain amount of energy during a sitting and the circle guides need to use the energy to develop the phenomena and practice it in their own vibration, before producing it in ours for us to experience. It is a reason why many circles break up, because patience and dedication is required in abundance. Sitters can believe that if every sitting doesn't produce results in our vibration that clearly the circle will not succeed. I always teach that when you dedicate yourself to this work, you should come together with intentions of enjoying each other's company for the evening and if spirit can produce some phenomena then it is an added bonus. Even well- developed circles have evenings when guides are unable to communicate. Conditions such as weather or illness have a huge impact on energy and vibrations.

A young man called Ben approached us. Terry and I knew him, a nice bubbly young lad who had good intentions and was very likeable. He asked if he could join the circle. Our numbers by this stage were greatly reduced and on most sittings were me, Terry and Sarah, so again we agreed he could sit on a trial basis. He met Sarah and they seemed to get on well at first.
Gradually over the next few weeks though, the harmony seemed to be compromised for two reasons. Firstly Sarah, who was a very well educated lady, seemed to become intolerant to Ben who was not an academic in any sense but brought humor to the circle; she became rather sarcastic in her tone towards him and at times belittled him too. Secondly, I had started to notice that if a circle sitting was quiet, Sarah would come out of circle and declare the evening had been a waste of time. She was very much still grieving and needed to have a sign in circle that her partner was close to her. I know when phenomena occurred it was of course the circle guides, but her mind told her it was her partner and it brought her much relief.

I began to feel anxious on the days of sitting and would pace for several hours beforehand, in case I let Sarah down. The more anxious I became the more the guides were unable to draw close with the group, the phenomena ground to a halt completely, a cycle had evolved, and I didn't know how to resolve it as Sarah had become a friend.

A very close friend of mine who is a fellow medium suggested I ask the guides to help me find a resolution. That night before I slept I sent a prayer asking for assistance. The following morning I was awake with the birds and feeling hopeful, I showered and dressed and was at my computer before 9am. I was surprised to see an e-mail waiting in my inbox for me, it was from Sarah. It was quite a lengthy correspondence, but basically it was a thank you for allowing her to join the circle but she felt at this time she needed to step out. I wrote a basic reply back to her, thanking her for her time and assuring her that an invitation as a guest would be extended to her when she had allowed enough time for the healing process of bereavement to have taken place. So that situation was resolved.

Sadly in the September John passed to the higher side of life and Alex moved abroad. So, the circle became three and the development continued forward. I won't bore you the reader with a lot of the circle entries in the logbooks, but just simply transcribe the more evidential sittings that we experienced, to show the progression that the circle guides made.

28th May 2006

Terry wrote: I felt strong vibrations from the start of the sitting, then saw a figure of someone sat on the floor, cross legged, between the table and the cabinet. I saw a faint light appearing in the same position at head height, illuminating the figure. I heard dripping (caused by ectoplasm) and a tapping noise on the stereo, a woman's voice was mumbling just above the stereo too. It was very hazy in the room and someone was clapping to the music. Jo wrote: A guide came close very quickly tonight, and there was movement around my chair and something solid touching me. It was very cold in the room and cabinet this evening.

Ben wrote: I saw a figure sat on the floor, crossed legs and a light appeared at the same time then disappeared. Lights shot around the room, the room was hazy too.

31st May 2006

Terry wrote: As soon as I had done the opening prayer I had a tingling sensation over my feet and up my legs. Dripping was heard in the cabinet (ectoplasm). Spirit lights started floating all around the ceiling and the table was rocking from side to side. Then I heard voices talking and a metallic sound.

Jo wrote: Lots of pulling around my neck tonight, again the guide came in very quickly this evening.

Ben wrote: A white light passed in front of me, heard lots of chatter and spirit lights close to the ceiling.

11th June 2006

Terry wrote: I saw lights appearing in the cabinet and a figure walked in front of me, causing a breeze as it did so. Lots of spirit lights all around the floor.

Jo wrote: I am still recovering from my operation and I felt extremely hot at the end of the sitting (maybe I was being given healing?)

Ben wrote: The cabinet kept lighting up with spirit lights and a figure walked in front of Terry and me.

So even at this early stage materialization was starting to reveal itself; the spirit lights at times would give a fascinating display, or be used to self- illuminate spirit forms.

2nd July 2006

Terry wrote: I saw lots of spirit lights around the cabinet and around Ben. Then I saw something coming out of the cabinet about three feet long and shaped like a rod. It was traveling towards the trumpet.

Jo wrote: Lots of wetness around my mouth? And I was very hot at the end of the sitting again.

Ben wrote: Something strange was coming out of the cabinet tonight, and I kept hearing a clicking noise, like someone flicking their nails.

3rd July 2006 A strange occurrence at bedtime

I woke up this morning, having had an unusual experience before dropping off to sleep last night. I was lying on my stomach after saying prayers, and very relaxed almost to the point of drifting off to sleep, when I suddenly became aware of a man's breathing in the room, somewhere at the foot of my bed. I raised my head and

looked in the direction it was coming from but could see nothing. I acknowledged aloud that I could hear him.
I placed my head back on my pillow but the breathing became even louder, again I raised my head but still could see nothing. I replaced my head, but the breathing became louder still.
I climbed to the bottom of my bed and suddenly saw coming from the top of my TV, almost what looked like a beam that went up and past my ceiling. I checked for any source that could be creating this by natural means, but could not account for it. After about a further minute, the beam disappeared and the breathing stopped.

For those of you that have read 'Spirit in the Physical' you will be well aware of these cylindrical tubes that Red Cloud spoke of, and you would also have seen the photograph that we believe captured this phenomena. Was this one of the same? Was this beam one of these cylindrical tubes that carries sounds between the vibrations? I shall never know the answer to that question for sure, but I think it is highly likely.

30th September 2006 during the night

I woke up about 3.15 am as my text on my phone woke me. After replying I settled back down, lying on my stomach. I had a feeling of coldness around my feet and was aware the tops of my arms stiffening up. I must have dropped back off to sleep but I awoke again sometime later feeling panicked and disorientated, as I could not feel the bed. I was aware of being extremely cold and my feet felt very full. I know that is a strange statement to make but it really does describe how they felt. I was then sat upright at the foot of my bed having been placed there. I couldn't work out initially where I was. Was this my first experience of levitation? Well I think it was my first conscious experience of levitation, but I suspect the guides had been practicing previously while I slept!

During much of the latter part of 2006, the circle only sat ad hoc. There were major changes going on in our personal lives and the harmony was lost for a period of time, while these changes took place.
In early 2007 the circle members changed because private issues were still causing problems. I was by this time also fostering a teenage lad, called Jason, who had become homeless in our village; he happened to be a friend of my sons so we knew him well. He had a huge interest in spiritual matters and was very keen to join the circle. He had wonderful energy and was intrigued by all the phenomena that happened spontaneously in my home, and yet had no fear of it at all.

26th February 2007

A friend of Jason's called around to see him, and as often happened we ended up having a table tilting session in my dining room. The table was very active and eventually tried to go through the doorway towards the séance room. Jason said, "I think they want us to invite Callum in there". So, we ended up in the séance room.

Now because there had been many problems with the circle sitters, I had been throwing my thoughts out to the guides to bring us another sitter. I don't believe in coincidences and I felt strongly that this young person Callum had been guided to work with us.

Jason, Callum, my son Jamie and me all entered the séance room and after saying a prayer and putting the light out we sat holding hands. No music was played or singing undertaken and after about a minute a bright strip of light shot at an angle from the ceiling down towards my right side. The table, which was not being touched by any of us, started to move about and rock against the sitters legs. Loud bangs were heard all over the walls as if being thumped by a fist. The trumpets which were stood on the floor in one corner of the room rose into the air and the metal one was taken around the circle touching each sitter on the head in turn. The other trumpet made from plywood moved around the circle touching each sitter on the knee. There were several things on the table and amongst them was a handkerchief; I asked the guides if they could possibly tie a knot in it, or write their name in chalk on the wall. They placed one of the trumpets on the table and began dragging it in a circular motion at an extremely fast pace; the noise was deafening.

Again the table was taken against the sitters' legs and tilted on its side. I asked the guides to hold all the objects on the table so that they did not fall, and this was carried out by them. When we put the light on at the end of this short session, the hanky had a knot in it and the name 'Kathleen' had been chalked on the wall.

I met a lovely gentle soul called Andrew; he was a single parent of a young son, and being a single parent myself, we had quite a connection and an understanding of each other's daily lives. There was no romantic attachment between us, just good friendship.
Andrew, having a big pull towards all things spiritual, joined our circle for a short while, but he was quite timid and fragile so did not stay long as he was of a nervous disposition.

2nd April 2007

We didn't normally sit on Mondays, but Andrew had childcare issues and so we moved from Friday to a Monday sitting to accommodate him. After opening prayers, we placed the two trumpets on the floor along with the chalk. The table rose a few inches into the air, came back down, then rose again but this time much higher. There were several wooden rings on the table, and I asked if it were possible for matter to be passed through matter, by linking two of the wooden rings together. My head felt like it had thick treacle on it; it felt like it was running down and trickling down onto my chest and into my lap. A faint whistle could be heard, which grew in strength the more we encouraged it. It continued for some five minutes then I asked the spirit responsible (a small child) to move to the other side of the room towards another sitter but the whistle grew weaker, so I asked for the spirit to come back and stand at my side again and the whistle grew much louder again. (Independent direct voice was developing at a pace now).

10th April 2007

It was just me, Jason and Callum tonight. The light phenomena very much manifested at this sitting as you will see, and gave us an insight into things to come. On several occasions during this sitting a light was seen to keep resting on the top of my head, followed by a glowing ball of light to my left; inside the ball of light was two eyes and a pointed beard of a gentleman. It appeared to be the image of one of our circle guides 'William'.

I have always been quite scientific in my approach to the paranormal, and it is well documented that like attracts like; we draw to us those on spirit side with similar outlooks. William was a scientist, a chemist to be precise. He also investigated the mediumship of Florence Cook and Daniel Dunglas Home and proclaimed the existence of a psychic force as fact. It made sense to me that this truly wonderful and wise soul would choose to assist us in our endeavours, but I have to say extremely humbling too, for who am I but an ordinary woman living in a country village. So these balls of light, or cylindrical tubes, indeed were capable of carrying the images of those on spirit side. Further development came later.

15th April 2007

We began this evening with table tilting, then moved to the séance room and took our usual places around the table, holding hands and ensuring that none of us were touching the table. The table began to move and tilt, spirit firmly held the objects in place including the trumpet. The hanky was picked up and dragged across each sitter's hands and then it was gently wafted in my face before being placed in my lap, then it was lifted once again and was taken to each sitter and placed over their hands, allowing each of us to be able to feel the materialised hand controlling the hanky. The trumpet then began to rise into the air, and was carried towards the ceiling, it stayed by the ceiling for some five or six seconds, before descending and touching each of us on the head. It was then waved in front of our faces before being placed back onto the table. William then turned his attention to the paper, touching us all with it, then screwing it up into balls and throwing them at us. He picked up the tambourine from a spare chair where it had been placed and started banging loudly on it in mid- air above the table. He then started to write on the wooden table with chalk; later we discovered he had written his name 'William'.

I then felt his hand on mine, feeling each finger and fully formed nail; his touch was incredibly firm but tender. His hand was much warmer than the usual body temperature on this side of life and there was an aroma, which I find difficult to describe, but the smell remained until the end of the sitting. He continued to allow me to hold his hand and took a great deal of time allowing me to grasp his hand firmly in mine. I could feel his knuckles and fingers and nails in great detail. He put his fingers through mine so that our palms touched. I was wearing a bracelet made from beads on a piece of elastic. William started to slip my hand out of my bracelet then put it back on me, then he raised my arm high above my head and slipped his hand through the bracelet too, so that his hand rested on my elbow. I could feel the length of his arm against mine. He then gently stroked my face. He moved around the table and touched Jason and Callum as well, but they were not allowed to grasp his hand as I had been permitted to do. William came back to me and tenderly stroked my hand before we said goodnight for the evening.

Ectoplasm has quite a pungent smell in early development but the smell does ease when sufficient development has taken place. It is also of note that ectoplasmic forms are attached to the medium, hence why it is safe in the initial stages for the medium to be able to touch manifested forms but not safe for others to do so, unless given permission by the circle guides.

Evidence from my Dad

My mother occupied herself during the weeks that
followed my father's passing, clearly having too much
time on her hands, and not wanting at that stage to sit
and dwell too much. She filled her days with sorting and
cleaning cupboards. One day she emptied all the contents
of the bathroom cabinet. It is a small cupboard, which
hangs on the wall and is airtight. She gave it a thorough
clean, sorted it contents before closing it and moving on
to the next one on her hit list. The following day was not a
good day for Mum, with frequent tearful episodes, which
resulted in her having a headache. She went to the
bathroom cabinet to get some pain killers, and on
opening the airtight cupboard, found a large white feather
neatly placed on the shelf; this instantly made her smile!

A week later she had a friend staying with her, they went shopping, and happened to see a sign for clairvoyant readings; they both decided to enter the building to book in for one. Readings were excellent, however one of the first things that my Dad said to my Mum through the medium was, "I brought you a feather to ease your pain."

Bless him.

The Residential Home

I have been a carer, mostly working in the community, for many years. I find it highly rewarding but physically exhausting at times.

A few years ago, I decided to move away from community work and spend time working in a residential home, initially providing the daily activities to its residents, but then finding them always short- staffed, I took on care duties too, often working from 8am until 10pm at night. The home was fairly old and very scruffy on the inside, but the food was good, and although needing a lick of paint, the home was kept clean.

At the end of the evening shift before handing over to the night staff, we had to write an account of each resident about how their day had been, in their care plans. This was the best part of the evening shift, as it allowed us time to sit, enjoy a coffee and chat while completing our tasks.

One evening we were sat in the small lounge writing the care plans when footsteps were heard in the corridor just outside the room. A colleague went to see which of the residents was up and wandering, only to find no one about, so she came back and sat down, saying that was weird and dismissed it.

The next day I was again on the late shift but this time with a different colleague, when again a strange noise from the corridor was heard. This time it sounded like something being dragged up the hallway. We both looked at each other and headed towards the hall, but neither of us could find a resident out of their bed or anything to account for the noise.

A few days later, again more disturbances, in the form of whispers in the hallway, and again on checking to see who was about, we found nothing.
Some of the care staff were beginning to think that the home was haunted, and becoming a little unnerved by it.

These disturbances continued to happen for many weeks, until one day one of the carers said, "I find it rather strange that we only get these disturbances when we are working with Jo!" I was a little embarrassed to be honest but was reluctant to tell them of my development as a physical medium. I didn't think they would understand the subject matter, and besides the cook had previously said to me, on returning from a funeral, "You know it's such a shame that if that family wanted to get a message from beyond the grave, they won't be able to now". On enquiring why she had made such a statement she replied, "Well their relative has been cremated, and you can only communicate if you're buried" !! I explained at length, that was not the case at all, as once you leave your body it is just an empty shell, and it is not required after you pass, so it makes little difference what happens to it.

The disturbances in the home continued, but they escalated to the point of care staff seeing apparitions on occasions in the corridors and hearing whispers close to their ears when entering certain rooms. I saw various spirit forms gliding down the corridors so I knew it was not a figment of their imaginations.

On one occasion we had a very poorly lady, who we were providing palliative care for, and we kept popping into her room every thirty minutes or so, to make sure she was comfortable, not in pain, and to moisten her lips. On entering her room for about the fourth time one evening, all the pictures on her walls were hanging the wrong way up; they had been turned completely around. She passed from this world the following day.

On another occasion, I was working with a colleague who had gone to the kitchen to make the coffee, before we settled down to write care plans. A few moments later she came into the lounge as white as a ghost and said that something had happened in the kitchen. I followed behind her and on entering the kitchen found all the cupboard doors and kitchen drawers open and the entire cutlery had been laid neatly in a row on the work surface, and there was a lot of cutlery indeed. We were the only staff members on duty and had been for several hours; all residents were asleep in their rooms, so there was no ordinary explanation other than a paranormal one to account for it.

I had not considered the possibility of spirit using my physical energy in my place of work, but I guess it does make sense.

Physical energy travels wherever I go, and is wherever I am, so the spontaneous phenomena can happen at any time and in any place.

I think there would have been some pretty relieved members of staff, when I left the home and returned to working in the community!

The Circle of Friends continues

The guides continued to materialize in the circle, walking amongst us in solid form, touching us, talking to us, sometimes using the trumpet and producing direct voice, and at other times by independent direct voice. Self-illuminating lights grew in strength and diameter and we were experiencing some wonderful phenomena, however our desire was for spirit forms to be walking and talking in full view amongst us.

Intentions of what you wish and hope to desire plays a big part in circle development, and I was told by a very wise soul, a number of years ago now, that what spirit have once achieved they can achieve again. I am not quite sure why and when total darkness was introduced into the séance room; it certainly was not like that a hundred years ago and I absolutely knew that spirit, like us, continue to evolve and develop new techniques of working, in light of the fact that our modern day scientists are passing to the higher realms and taking with them, their knowledge of our modern day living and modern day technology.

We decided that it was time to introduce light back into our séance room. We experimented with red light, blue light, dim white light and candle light; the phenomena seemed temporarily to grind to a halt, had we made a mistake? Most of the phenomena had always happened spontaneously in ordinary daylight before I had actually focused my energy for the development of this mediumship, so why had the phenomena stopped?

What we did not realize was that when new conditions are introduced or even sometimes new sitters, the energy in the room changes completely. The guides have to work under a completely different set of conditions and often it can take the development back to the very beginning! Our sittings changed in format; it took longer to build the vibrations in the room, more water had to be drunk to stop us really feeling dehydrated, and we felt fatigued often when coming out of circle.

The change we had made by introducing light was having a physical impact on us, and we had the easy job of just sitting and enjoying each other's company. Goodness knows how that affected the guides and there work. It took several months of perseverance and dedication before results started to be seen once again. The ectoplasm had become tolerant to light for very short periods of time initially, but it showed us that the guides had been working extremely hard to move the circle forward in its development.

It was direct voice that started again first, whistles actually, then words and so on. The ectoplasmic voice box was also seen for the first time, which was fascinating for onlookers, of course with it being attached to my throat and sitting on my shoulder. I was reliant on seeing photographs of it.

I am often asked what physical effects I feel from it, if indeed I do feel any at all. Well, yes I do, generally I am unable to turn my head; it feels a bit like having a surgical collar on, my shoulder aches, not particularly painfully, and of course instant relief is felt the moment the voice box is withdrawn. When the voice box is being used by a spirit communicator, the back of my neck feels like it is vibrating and a sensation at my throat like pulling on strings, but of course the voice box is an ectoplasmic mirror image of the mediums vocals and it is attached to the actual vocal chords which they twang on to create the sound. At the same time they pass air through the mechanics of the voice box to be able to produce the sound. It is a highly complicated procedure as I understand it, but once the voice box has been built, which can take many months or even years, it is a much easier process for them to create each sitting.

You will also see throughout this book, photographs, the majority of which were taken during circle sittings. The use of cameras has also been a priority, to enable us to bring tangible evidence to a greater audience. However, it must be noted that flash photography is prohibited, as ectoplasm can still retract at a pace, if exposed to excessive or sudden bright light.

The majority of this chapter has been dictated to me by William, through my clairaudience; we try to be as accurate as we can in our details and scientific explanations, but there is still much to learn.

A very Special Séance

Sunday 28th April 2013 proved to be a very special day.
I had invited some friends over to my house, so there
were three guests, plus me and Terry the circle leader.
Keeping their identities protected I will call the guests
Jane, Elaine and Richard. Elaine and Richard were
partners. All have sensitivities to spirit in varying degrees.

My guests arrived within minutes of each other and were
very excited at the invitation; lots of laughter and chatter
began to build energy even before we entered the séance
room.
Richard, who often holds workshops, had brought some
items at my request, to place in the séance room; a
Victorian brass doorknocker that had simply been
mounted on to a piece of wood, and what was referred to
as a light box. This small device was a bulb that would be
used for a car headlamp. It sat on the outside of a wooden
box, alongside a switch; this was connected to a battery
inside the box. The idea of the gadget was for spirit
operators to turn the light bulb on and off at their
pleasure or as they required. Richard stated that it had
not been successful at his events previously but was
hopeful that spirit operators in a physical circle such as
ours could operate the device. We placed both objects in
the séance room, where they would be in full view of all
sitters, and left the room.

About fifteen minutes later we were all preparing to enter
the séance room for the sitting. Terry the circle leader
was first to enter and as he did so, he spoke aloud saying,
"Hello guides, are you ready for us"? The doorknocker
began to knock, untouched by human hands. The red
light lit the room quite brightly so we could see the

doorknocker being lifted and knocked quite vigorously. We all chuckled as we filed into the room and sat down.

Terry had placed the spirit trumpet on the table, alongside pen and paper, as the guides often wish to bring messages and drawings through direct writing. Direct writing differs from automatic writing in one very significant way; unlike automatic writing, which requires the use of the medium's hand, direct writing is produced by spirit manifesting and picking up the writing implement for themselves. Sometimes they completely manifest, and at other times when the psychic power is low, they manifest only a hand.

We sat in a semi- circle with the two men at each end. The table was two to three feet in front of us. Richard sat next to me, Jane sat to my left, then Elaine, and finally Terry. Elaine and Jane were both quite nervous so I suggested holding hands might help them to remain calm, so we all linked hands. We had been playing music before we sat to raise the vibrations in the room; we switched it off and said an opening prayer. Immediately the bulb on the light box lit up, we turned off the red light, the doorknocker began to knock once again. Then the light box went out and we were plunged into darkness albeit the light coming from the luminous tabs on the trumpet.

My head started to feel floaty which is an indicator that levitation is about to occur; sure enough the sitter Richard seated next to me was lifted into the air. The feeling of levitation is a strange one. Some are under the impression that an ectoplasmic rod is used as in the Goligher Circle of many years ago. However, in our circle, the person being lifted feels the fingertips on their arms, of those manifested in the room, and are lifted as a child would be lifted by its mother.

Richard was brought back down in a controlled manner but in all was carried into the air some eight times during this séance. Richard understands the personal evidence from those in spirit, so his interest lies in the power of spirit, meaning, what they can achieve in our vibration, so the phenomena aspect of physical mediumship is very important to him.

We sang our 'happy song' and the knocker began to knock once more, and the trumpet, which was standing on the table, began to rise into the air. Clearly, someone had manifested in the room, as we could hear loud stomping all over the floor from what sounded like feet.

The trumpet, which was now in front of me suspended in mid-air, began to move rapidly and was carried to the ceiling. I called out, "Hello there, have you manifested"? A man's voice replied, "Yes" through the trumpet, which was being used as an amplifier. Jane and Elaine, who had never heard a spirit voice speak before, seemed quite alarmed. Terry reassured them that there was nothing to fear from our friends and that they came with pure love.

The man started to call to Terry, his voice was fairly weak initially, but then seemed to grow in strength. Terry asked him for his name, and "Johnny, Johnny", he said. It was Terry's father who had been in spirit some sixteen years; his father was an Irishman and was a devout Catholic, so I know he would have found communicating very difficult. Terry's father tried hard to speak and indicated that Terry's mother was with us too in the room. It was a very emotional reunion between them.

Johnny placed the trumpet back on the table when he had finished speaking to Terry, but before leaving he promised he would return to circle again and that he would attempt to write a message on the paper through direct writing as further proof of him manifesting. Moments later the paper on the table began to rustle and the pen was tapped several times to indicate that he had picked it up. The sound of a pen writing on paper could be heard, then the paper was carried through the air ; we could hear it flapping about and placed beside Terry on the floor, the light box was switched on again by spirit, and there lay two pieces of paper. One was signed by Terry's father; he verified his father's writing and signature, but also his father had written Terry's name on it and it was spelt differently to how we always spell the name (Tery). Terry confirmed that his father had always spelt his name this way. The other piece of paper contained rather large writing; it simply said, 'Love mum x'. This was the first time Terry's parents had communicated in our séance room.

Spirit started to knock on the doorknocker again and we jokingly said, come on in, they switched the light off again, and we began singing our happy song once more, while Terry composed himself.

A couple of minutes later footsteps were heard again across the room and the trumpet was lifted high into the air;, again a man's voice with an accent began to call out, and he called to me, "Jo." I responded that I could hear him and asked who he was. "I protect you", he said, "I am White Eagle". I was overcome with emotion. I had seen White Eagle on numerous occasions, but he was one of the circle guides who had not previously spoken. His voice was strong and soothing, as he spoke to me and others in the room. He held my hand and stroked my fingers with such tenderness. He thanked me for working in this way and promised that he has and always would keep me safe and those that came to the circle. Jane who was sat next to me asked if he would chant for us before he stepped back, which he did with a lyrical voice. He gave us a blessing before stepping back and placing the trumpet back on to the table. The weather conditions on that evening had been very unsettled and I believe that's why they were using the trumpet to amplify their voices rather than speak without it, or maybe it was to satisfy Richard's need for phenomena.

We again started to sing our happy song, and moments later the trumpet rose again, footsteps were heard in front of me and Jane, and a woman started to call to Jane. Jane responded that she could hear her and asked her to identify herself, as she didn't recognize her voice. "I am Jenny your guide", she said. Jane became very emotional as she has worked for spirit herself as a clairvoyant for many years and had not received any personal confirmation from her guide previously, other than through a mental link. Jenny exchanged kind words of gratitude for her dedication and they spoke for some ten minutes. Jane said to Jenny that she would have to leave the séance room as the energy was making her feel quite sick. Jenny replied,"Stay please, stay please, I will remove the sickness for you, sit perfectly still", and then Jane had Jenny's solid hand placed upon her stomach; instantly the nausea left her.
Jenny moved towards the table and again we could hear the rustle of paper and the pen writing, and the paper flapping in mid- air was moved towards Jane. Jenny said, "For you", and retreated. Immediately spirit put the light on again and there was writing, a note for Jane from Jenny. Jane was so overcome with emotion at this point,

she had heard her guide speak with her, received a hand-written note and been touched by her manifested guide!

Jenny had replaced the trumpet back on the table before leaving, so we again began to sing our happy song. Within moments the trumpet rose again and footsteps were heard walking across the floor, this time another woman was calling to Elaine. I think the experience had been overwhelming for Elaine, as she was giggling uncontrollably at this point and was laughing when she responded. The energy can have that effect on some people; others like Jane have feelings of nausea.

Elaine asked the female who she was and she responded with, "Marina, your guide". Elaine spoke to her guide about the power of crystals and in particular her love of aquamarine, to which Marina said she already knew. They spoke about very diverse subjects even mermaids, which I found quite bizarre, however we each have different needs which are recognized by our guides, and which attracts those that choose to work with us. Marina and Elaine spoke for several minutes, before Marina bid us all farewell.

Marina replaced the trumpet on the table, the doorknocker began to knock again and we all watched it by the light of the bulb from the light box. We began to sing our happy song again which is incidentally: if you're happy and you know it, clap your hands. Very simple but perfect for harmony amongst sitters.
Spirit turned off the light again, and again the trumpet rose into the air, footsteps were heard walking across the floor to Terry, and loud chanting could be heard. Elaine began to giggle again when a male voice suddenly shouted for her to stop, and it made her jump. The voice of

another Indian was heard calling to Terry. Terry responded by saying, "I can hear you friend, who are you?" "I'm the chief", he said, "your guide". His voice seemed to boom more than the others before him. They spoke at length about healing and channeling healing, as this guide was a great healer himself when on this side of life. Elaine was still giggling somewhat as the energy in the room was growing more in strength. When the chief withdrew several minutes later, I suggested maybe Jane and Elaine leave the séance room to take a break, whilst me, Terry, and Richard remained alone. They readily agreed and went to prepare some refreshments for the group.

We began to sing again our happy song, the door knocker was knocking vigorously, and then suddenly a manifestation was seen by us all floating above our heads, a large figure that seemed be to self -illuminated. It moved across the room before dematerializing. I think if Elaine and Jane had been present it may well have been too much for them to absorb; the evening had already been very enlightening to them. Richard was mesmerized by it all and was not at all unnerved.

We believe the figure floating above our heads was Dan, a circle guide and a physical medium here on the earth plane. Known more commonly to all of you as D D Home, amongst his phenomena through his mediumship was levitation.
And so, the work moves forward with phenomena in good light and self-illumination too.

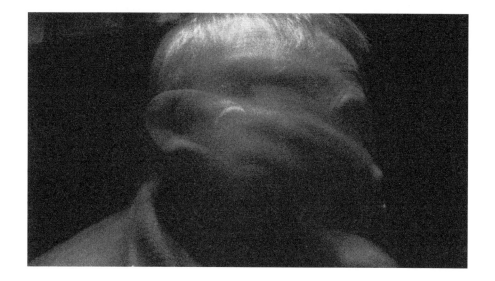

The Skype Experiments

I have a very good friend, Norman, who has been researching the paranormal for well over thirty years. He has written books on his findings and was the author of my first book, Spirit in the Physical.

We were in constant contact, almost daily, and discuss all issues regarding this fascinating subject. It came as no surprise to him, when one morning I felt inspired to embark on an experiment with his help.
It involved sitting under red light conditions in my séance room and using Skype, in an experiment to see if transfiguration and direct voice could be achieved using modern technology to transmit it.

A few years ago, during the trance sitting with Red Cloud (transcribed in Spirit in the Physical), he foretold a journey of development that lay ahead of me. I am astounded to report all that he spoke of has come to pass. He spoke of a veil of ectoplasm, and voice, translated meaning transfiguration accompanied by direct voice. I am blessed to have developed in both these areas. However, of late I have tried to push the boundaries within physical mediumship and have been pondering on how many people could access the true power of spirit, when they don't have access to a physical medium.
Was I inspired? Maybe, but the experiment brought results I was not expecting.

The experiments took place over twelve sittings in April 2013. A family member, Jackie, was staying with me for a couple of weeks holiday. She proved to be a real asset, as she assisted us in experimenting with the new technique of working. The sittings took place in my séance room.

My laptop was placed on the table in front of me. To my left was a lamp with a 40 watt red bulb. Jackie was sat opposite me at the table; she had my digital camera with the flash disabled, but it did still have red eye in use. Norman was at his home, in his lounge. He had set his video camera up pointed at his computer screen. It was on a tripod to avoid handshake.

We both connected to Skype, and made adjustments so that a clear view could be seen and recorded on the video. Neither of us had any expectations of good results, but we were still careful to record the proceedings as accurately as possible.

The ectoplasmic voice box generally sits on my right hand side of my neck and shoulder, so we kept the lamp to the left of me as ectoplasm can be very intolerant of light, but there remained good light in order to see the area clearly. On the first sitting it took only a couple of minutes, before the ectoplasm gathered and started to form the tube that sits on the side of my neck; it looks a little like a large swollen neck tendon that runs up behind the ear. The remainder of the voice box mechanics formed on my shoulder, and looked rather like a mass or lump. It could be seen constantly swirling and changing shape and was dark in color.

Jackie who was sat opposite me with the camera, started to take a few photographs, remarking to Norman that she would take shots each time she saw the phenomena happening, and would not just take random photographs, as they would hold no evidential value at all. Norman agreed and said physical mediumship has to be seen in order to be classed as physical, with the exception of spirit photography, which traditionally is spirit extras in photographs. Norman also remarked that he wanted to match up the still photographs to the video footage at the end of each of the sittings.

I was sat in a very relaxed state, semi -meditative but not entranced. I was aware of all the conversations taking place and even interjected where necessary. Most people believe that trance is required for physical phenomena including transfiguration and direct voice, but whilst it is true some mediums do need to be in this state of consciousness, others like me do not. It is dependent on the level of development that has taken place. I have always been extremely lucky to experience direct voice in daylight conditions as well as séance conditions.
The first sitting lasted about twenty minutes; I could hear Jackie and Norman being very excited at the results, in particular with the way it was established that the ectoplasm was tolerant to be video being recorded and photographed.

Jackie stated that she could see a blue substance oozing from my ear; she could see it clearly and photographed it. It appeared to be separate from the ectoplasm. On checking the photographs afterwards, it seemed to be a vibrant blue. Spirit were encouraged to try to make sounds; we knew that spirit had a lot of obstacles to overcome with all the technology to master, however we started to hear a loud screeching noise coming from the speakers and the occasional sound that resembled words.

After the sitting, Norman uploaded the video and sent me a link to watch, which I did later that day. I was quite amazed at the results. Norman being an ex- scientist, started to evaluate the evidence from the sitting. Part of that evaluation was to try and eliminate ordinary explanations for any or all that had been witnessed and experienced. Here is his written report of that sitting.

Skype (1) 14th April 2013

'The first video'd sitting showed at first Jo's neck throbbing and a raised structure like a tube going partly up the neck. Jo shut her eyes and was silent for a while. At 46 seconds there was an irregular sound which we began calling 'screeching', which covers different sounds and patterns of sounds over the speakers. From 1.32 to 1.40 there was a kind of whistling screech, as always hard to describe unless you hear it. There was more screeching from 1.50 - 2.57 when it stopped abruptly. Jo's face was misty especially around her mouth. Screeching from 3.16 - 3.46, sounded a bit like Morse code. All these screeches were different from each other. At 4.30 there was a rattling kind of screech. Tappings were heard at 4.46. Jo then came awake and looked at Jackie's photos. They showed a vibrant blue on her. Jackie saw Jo's face changing. Photos showed what appeared to be a voice box on Jo's right neck area, which she saw in the room at the time of taking the photos, and it's seen on the video. Jo asked 'them' for speech, and she saw my web camera zooming in and out on me, though I had not moved at all. The tube was still very prominent on Jo's neck at 13.23. I asked for confirmation that this was a real paranormal experience, and there was a rap at 15.50. Jackie saw a vibrant blue color on the right side of Jo's face, which was captured on a photo, and her photos showed blue on Jo's hands.

I asked my son to watch the video and suggest ways in which it could all have happened normally with no spirit contact. He is independent and a sceptic. His comments:

'He did not think the sounds were feedback from all the electronic equipment, or produced by me or Jo as they had a pattern or rhythm, which changed, therefore had to be produced by 'someone'. The throbbing neck might indicate a voice box, but did Jo and Jackie hear it in the room separately from the speaker's sound, as is traditional? Theoretically, Skype can be hacked into, sceptics might claim it's a joke played on us. He thought that fraud by Jo or confederates was the most likely explanation, as hacking would be very difficult and they would have to know when we were on Skype then hack in with the screech sounds as they watched and listened. Software is available which records directly onto the PC hard disc that which is seen and heard on Skype, eliminating any other cause after it goes out from Jo. There is no mechanism for sound waves to go from a silent voice box through Jo's microphone through Skype internet through my PC, through my speakers, so I can hear it this end.

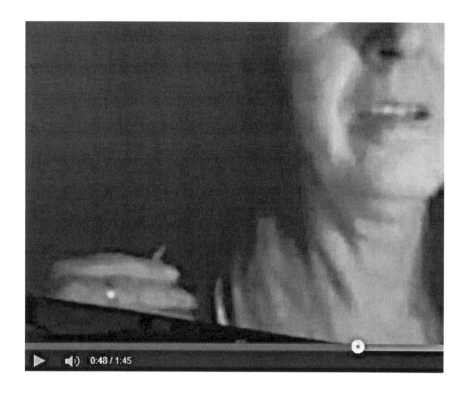

I researched photos of voice boxes. A Margery Crandon photo showed a tube from her nose to her right shoulder, and a formation there well away from her neck. A Leslie Flint photo shows a mass on his left shoulder but a tube can't be seen. Jack Webber can be seen with a tube from his right ear to a mass on his shoulder. These masses thought to be ectoplasm were all similar in appearance on the shoulder. It seemed a good idea to try to photograph and video Jo's shoulder as well as the neck, to see what the whole structure looked like.

Norman also consulted a friend of his, who was an expert in light rays. He wanted to know if the computer or lamp or both could cause the production of the blue substance; his opinion was, it would not.

The experiment continued each day, with more and more sounds and words being heard and recorded. The blue substance became more in quantity and showed that it worked side by side of the ectoplasm but it did not seem to mix. The ectoplasm continued to be concentrated around the neck and shoulder area, and Jackie continued to take still photographs of all the phenomena that she was witnessing first hand. Norman was experiencing phenomena himself during each sitting, that being with his recording equipment. We had noticed on the recordings that Norman's video camera on his computer kept zooming in and out on his profile, we found this quite amusing but there was no explanation to account for it, or certainly not one that came to mind.

We continued with the sittings and on the final sitting of the experiment at the end of April, the true evidence was brought to us. I had a bad headache that day and decided not to sit for more than a few minutes. Norman had been sending me healing and again the blue substance is clearly seen even more predominant though this time. I was wearing a cardigan, as I was feeling cold too. I exposed my shoulder to the camera; the voice box tube was throbbing on my neck, and the mass of ectoplasm that gathers on my shoulder seemed to have formed into what looked like a miniature head of an old gentleman.

This was a huge leap forward in just twelve days. I was keen to continue with this exciting experiment, however, Norman started experiencing severe problems with his PC even though it was only a few months old. He sent it to the repair shop but the specialist could find no reason for the machine breaking down. The saga continued for several weeks and Norman had to resort to using his old PC that he had stored away in his bedroom.

I feel there will be more to this experiment; it feels unfinished to me, so watch this space!

Physical effects on the body

If anyone had even made the slightest remark that
mediumship could have had a physical effect on the body,
I would have laughed at them.
But having read about my journey, you have learnt that it
truly does. Even mental mediumship has an impact, to a
much smaller degree than physical mediumship, but an
impact all the same.

One of the first signs that someone has psychic abilities is
the amount of static shocks that they experience; this
clearly is a physical impact on the body. I used to suffer
dozens each day, from the car, my fireplace, light
switches, even the shopping trolleys at my local
supermarket. They were very painful, I can tell you! Once
I started to use my psychic gifts they diminished.

Emotional changes are I guess the hardest to deal with.
Mood changes that sweep over you often without
warning. I know my own family were indeed confused at
times and probably believed I was having some sort of
mental break down. To be honest I thought I was
becoming mentally unstable myself, on more than one
occasion. I even sought reassurance from my doctor.
Sleep patterns are often disturbed; lack of sleep increases
the emotions, added to that when you're tired your
appetite decreases because you're too tired to prepare
food. Lack of food can make you cranky, so a bit of a cycle
evolves.

These emotional changes occur during all forms of
spiritual development, so no matter whether you are
developing clairvoyance, trance or physical, you can
expect high and low days. I am a strong believer that

knowledge is a powerful tool, so forewarned is forearmed. Of course this is not a long-term problem and generally will come and go as development takes place.

Trance tends to cause the most problems with the emotional state as I have previously stated, but it's not only the highs and lows, but also the feeling of invasion at times, what do I mean by this? Invasion of the mind and body. Spirit has to draw our attention to our sensitivities, and then it is a choice as to whether we wish to develop it. The beginning stages of trance or overshadowing as it should be correctly termed, requires spirit to blend with our minds, so our thoughts become muddled and cloudy, our bodies feel heavy as if weighted down, but there seems to be no other effective way of spirit actually being able to prove that one has the ability to be used in this way. Another sensitive can tell us, but generally all that does is leave us wondering if what we have been told, is true. Nothing can replace personal experience to give us definitive proof. Once that proof is brought to us and we choose to develop it further then a deeper connection is made by those in spirit. Physical manipulation of the body is one of the most difficult and uncomfortable effects, as the guide will often use the mediums vocal chords which can feel like pressure is being exerted on the throat and neck, but often wishes to use the mediums physical body too. Often the guide is seen over the medium during trance sessions. This effect involves the guide projecting his energy and blending it with the mediums energy. The guide does not jump into the medium's body; there is only one space for one soul in the physical body, but he does come very close in the auric field, giving a feeling that your body is housing him too. The body feels heavy and stretched. The more development that takes place, the more the medium is able to withdraw on a conscious level, the less the effects are felt. Deep trance can be achieved where no memory of the sitting or the words spoken can be recalled by the medium, but I have to stress it is very rare indeed for this level to be attained and would take many years to achieve. Most trance mediums can hear or feel at least some of what is taking place.

Trance development takes place at night too during our sleeping hours. Jerking of limbs is often experienced as the guide manipulates your energy field to assist in the control of trance. I often still find myself waking as a leg or arm jerks rapidly, but this is more than usual muscle jerking that can take place due to ordinary sleep movement.

I have already highlighted the feelings of nausea and the need to vomit during the highly sensitive stages of development with trance, and although it was troublesome for several months, I no longer suffer, which shows that as development progresses some effects are indeed short lived whilst others will stay with you for longer periods of time.

Physical mediumship brings a new set of physical effects on the body. You have to remember that a physical medium that works with ectoplasm is being used for the purpose of the substance, ectoplasm, to be withdrawn from him or her. The history books are filled with accounts of burns and internal injuries when this substance has been touched or exposed to excessive light. I received a nasty burn across my eyebrow due to the irresponsible act of a sitter, and although it had been caused by accident it was extremely painful.

Ectoplasm can be drawn from any bodily orifice, and in my case often from my tear ducts, but this leaves a residue, which hardens and is likened to sleep in the eye. It is gritty and often gets in my eyes in very small quantities. As a child, I was very troubled with styes, in fact I was rarely without one. One has to wonder if this was an early sign of ectoplasm being withdrawn and the physical effect on the body.

Also when guides practice on us during the sleep hours and ectoplasm is drawn from the mouth, it often results in choking; mine generally manifested in choking dreams as previously described.

The solar plexus is also a very popular withdrawal area for ectoplasm, and can leave tenderness on the body. Lots of water should be drunk before, during and after working on a physical level.

One final effect I should mention, although this is not an exhaustive list, is the increase in headaches and migraines particularly in unstable weather conditions and if you fail to properly rehydrate after opening to spirit. Also rehydrating properly can alleviate pain and discomfort, in or around the solar plexus.

Remember we are all individual instruments, each of us play a different tune, as each of us will experience physical effects differently. Your experiences may mirror my own or they may not resemble them at all. If in doubt always seek medical advice and always act responsibly when working on this level with spirit.

Workshops

I had been told by the spirit guides that I would be used as a teacher, so that I could pass on all that I had learnt during my journey to others that walked the same path. Of course we always hope what we are told is accurate in every detail, but until it actually comes to fruition, it is information that we store neatly in a compartment of our minds, while we await for the time of fulfillment.

In 2011, I had the good fortune to meet another medium called Gail. I met her through a good friend of mine, who had highly recommended that I make contact with her, as she ran an agency for all things spiritual. She has an excellent reputation but mostly for dealing with the darker side. What do I mean by the darker side? Hauntings, possessions, poltergeists, earth walkers and even voodoo cases. All of these things, I must highlight, are rare.
I spoke with Gail at length, about workshops on physical mediumship; she had little knowledge of the subject at the time, but was eager to trial one to see if they would be a popular addition to services that she could offer her clientele.

I set about doing lots of preparation and the first workshop took place. They were a lovely group of people that were all keen to learn more on the subject and to do practical work, in the hope of having an experience themselves. Which many of them did. We carried out experiments with table tilting, transfiguration, spirit photography, EVP, and a séance that day.
It was during an experiment with transfiguration and spirit photography that the greatest excitement came forth. I was sat at one side of the room and the attendees

were taking it in turn to be photographed by each other. Gail was in the kitchen preparing lunch for us all. I suddenly became aware that my mouth was speaking words, which were: "One of you is going to capture spirit in a minute". No sooner were the words spoken than an excited woman called out, that she had!

Her photograph contained what seemed to be etherialisation of two spirits and mysterious blue lights on my chest.

Etherialisations are vapourised spirit forms, produced from ectoplasm, but in far less quantity than would be needed for full form materialization.

All the students were amazed by the capture of these two spirit forms. On close inspection of the photograph, it also revealed spirits sitting in chairs as if observing the proceedings, but their faces were not clearly defined like the two in the center of the photograph.

Etherialisation can also be produced by spirit operators using a different method to the one with the photograph, and it was at a later workshop that this was demonstrated to the students. This time we were carrying out an experimental séance with a different group of students. The woman sat next to me remarked that I was looking rather strange and in fact not like myself at all, but had donned male features, which included a beard and moustache and a different hair style. Several photographs were taken to capture this form of etherialisation. In this method, spirit coat the mediums body with ectoplasm and mould it to form their own features; either form is highly evidential.

Transfiguration also produced some highly evidential experiences for numerous students, when sitting under red light conditions, and using the spirit cabinet to keep the energy concentrated close to the sitter. Varying degrees of transfiguration took place and I feel actually highlighted the gift to those that would be able to work with spirit in this way.

On one such occasion during a transfiguration experiment, communication was enhanced by the movement of the cabinet, which was spirit endorsed. They swayed the cabinet back and forth or side to side in answer to questions put to them. The sitters face became lumpy and his eye was blackened out by ectoplasm. On another occasion, the sitters face was completely blanked out by a swirling mist, vapourised ectoplasm, and on both occasions, photographs were taken to record the events.

Spirit also demonstrated elongation, first noted by the Victorian medium Daniel Dunglas Home (pronounced Hume). Several of my fingers were extended by about one and a half inches. D D Home used to exhibit this phenomenon but generally his torso was elongated by up to a foot. Some sitters were so shocked by this spectacular phenomenon that they would run from the room in horror.

Further phenomena, was that of independent direct voice. At nearly every workshop some direct voice was heard by those present, at times a soft whispering and at other times loud enough for someone to respond, believing it to be someone physically in the room. Independent direct voice is quite a rare phenomenon these days particularly in lit conditions, and especially when working with different people, rather than an established circle that has sat usually for many years.

The workshops are very popular and we received many requests to run a six-week course. So in response, we did. It was mostly experienced mediums that attended; some that had a physical circle already sitting and some that were looking into the possibility of opening a circle. The energy from week one was incredible, and I can say with complete honesty that egos were left at the door. The group, some of whom knew each other well, began to blend and harmonise, which is an important ingredient when working on a physical level. The group experienced some amazing phenomena within the six-week course and some reported that it was aiding their own circles too. We were careful to document the development through photographic evidence.

I am a strong believer that all forms of mediumship represents healing, so part of the course we dedicated to trance healing, with some showing the potential to be used for psychic surgery. However, psychic surgery is and probably always will be a controversial subject and so particular caution is needed when experimenting in this area.

The workshops hopefully have and do aid the development of many physical circles in the country, some sitting for the whole development of physical, and some sitting for a specialist area such as for the development of transfiguration. However, they also have given me the opportunity to flourish in a teaching role. I have learnt something new from every workshop from the lovely individuals that have attended; it has really highlighted that we are all individuals and develop at a different pace and in different ways. No two instruments are the same.

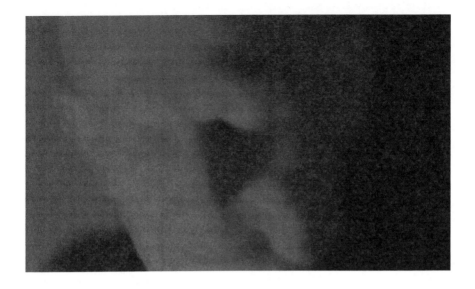

Spirit Photography

I find spirit photography very intriguing indeed. I have seen lots of photographs in books taken many years ago, in the heyday of spiritualism.

But what is spirit photography? Spirit photography became popular during the mid- 19th century with the introduction of film cameras, and the rise of Spiritualism. Deceased people mysteriously appeared in photographs (not orbs), the history books have many good examples of some genuine, and sadly some not.

Of late, it seems there are very few that introduce this phenomenon through their mediumship, my own development in this area being a relatively new one too. It was during a physical mediumship workshop that I was running with a friend and colleague, that my own sensitivity to this phenomenon first presented itself. I was both surprised and delighted at this new development. It highlighted to me, that we as mediums continue to evolve.

We were carrying out a transfiguration experiment at the workshop; two attendees were sitting in the open fronted cabinet. I was taking various photographs of them and the rest of the group. A red light sat next to the cabinet so that we could see any manifestation of spirit. I took several photographs of the ladies sitting in the cabinet, who happened to be sisters. I did not notice anything strange with the photographs until much later in the day. I had returned home from a very exhilarating day and uploaded the photographs on to my computer. It was during close inspection that I became aware of a small, Edwardian dressed lady, stood in the cabinet beside one of the sitters. I could clearly see all her features including her hair color. To anyone viewing the photograph they would believe she was actually attending the workshop, except for one detail, her size. She was perfect in every detail but was only about two feet tall!

I immediately contacted the sisters, and when they saw the photograph for themselves, declared the lady to be their auntie Flo, who had been in spirit for several years. I was amazed, and believing it to a one off event, I thanked spirit and put the experience to the back of my mind. However, several weeks later at another physical mediumship workshop, the experience was to be repeated . This time just the head of a man sporting a goatee and a full head of hair appeared between my colleague and another attendee. This time neither of them recognized the gentleman, which led me to question why spirit would take the trouble to reveal themselves in photographs without highlighting who they were connected to.

I am incredibly lucky that the spirit team that work with me generally respond quite quickly to my enquiring mind.

A couple of months later, during a six week course, another spirit extra appeared in a photograph, this time a gentleman with prominent features and wearing spectacles, revealed himself stuck to the back of my colleague's head. This highly amused me, but knowing my spirit team well, knew this was their way of responding to my previous question. Two weeks later, another spirit extra, but this time the gentleman had attached himself to the back of a female attendees head; she recognized him as her father.

I know many thousands of people regularly capture orbs in their photographs, but these were actual people, recognizable people that have all passed to the higher plane, so how was it possible to capture these wonderful souls and in such detail on my photographs?
Spirit guides explain the phenomena as another facet of physical mediumship. Ectoplasm can be used in various ways and often when a physical medium uses technology such as cameras, the guides will take the opportunity to withdraw ectoplasm so that those on the other side may utilize it for the purpose of creating their images on photographs.

So my understanding of this phenomena was growing, it needed a physical medium, ectoplasm and a camera, film or digital it made no difference according to the guides, and the spirit of a loved one wanting to draw close to the earth plane, to connect with someone here in the physical, in the presence of a physical medium. I was feeling rather pleased with myself and all that I was learning, but, and it's a big but, then came the twist that threw all my learning up in the air...

In August 2012, I ran a workshop in Basingstoke again with my colleague. Amongst the attendees was an ex - scientist who had been to previous events.
He received that day the most outstanding personal evidence through transfiguration and cabinet communication. A month later at another workshop that he did not attend, another spirit extra appeared on my photograph, a gentleman with a full head of hair and a beard. Nobody at the workshop recognized him, so I decided to upload the photograph and place it on my face book page. About half an hour later my telephone began to ring and on answering it, I heard quite a timid voice. It was the ex- scientist who said he had been pacing when he had seen my photograph of the spirit extra. He said he was really shocked as the image was of his deceased brother who had been in spirit for over ten years. He e-mailed me a photograph of his brother for comparison and indeed, it was his brother. But how could this be? He had not been at the workshop, so how could his brother have come through to project his image onto my photograph? Again, I turned to my spirit guides to seek the answer to my question.

Their explanation had been a simple one; my initial understanding had not been quite correct. Spirit do not require their loved one to be present to be photographed, although there would be little point from an evidential view point, unless as in the case with the ex- scientist they knew their image would reach the person they wished to connect with. They simply require a physical medium, a camera and ectoplasm.

I now have quite a portfolio of spirit extras and the development continues in this exciting area of my work.

An easy to Follow Guide For the Development of A Physical Circle

This chapter's purpose is more as a reference point that can be referred to, when you feel ready to set up a physical circle for development. I pass to you all that I learnt over the years, to give you the best possible chance of successful results and hopefully avoid the mistakes I made along the way.

So, what is a physical mediumship circle?

A circle that sits for the development of phenomena, that can be seen, heard, felt or smelt by more than one person.

How does spirit produce phenomena?

Through the use of a physical medium, ectoplasm, energy or a mixture of ectoplasm and energy.

Can anyone be a physical medium?

Sadly no, about one in every 100,000 has the right physicality to be used in this way; often when a circle forms, a physical medium has not be identified. Some circles will not succeed to produce physical phenomena that bring evidence of survival, but will experience paranormal activity. Some circles will experience no phenomena at all and some will change its intentions and divert to sit for another form of mediumship. Some circles sadly disperse.

The Environment

Ideally a room that can be kept strictly for the purpose of sittings, a spare bedroom is perfect, However, most people don't have the luxury of rooms that can be kept solely for development, so a room that is lockable and can be transformed into a peaceful space.

It should be free from as much technology as possible and what electrical equipment remains should be unplugged.

Mirrors should be removed as they can create vortexes.

The room should be kept at a comfortable temperature and be cleaned regularly.

Windows and doors should be blacked out with either blinds or curtains. Lighting should be introduced but under controlled conditions, so light sources seeping into the room from windows and doors must be avoided.

Seating should be comfortable with upright chairs, as in dining chairs rather than armchairs. If we become too comfortable, we can become less aware of changes in the room and can miss vital signs that are being brought forward by spirit.

The room should be as free from clutter as possible with one corner able to house an area for a spirit cabinet. The cabinet can be as basic as a curtain hung at an angle across the corner of the room and erected the day of the sitting and then stored away until the next sitting. My own cabinet was black lining material hung on a net curtain wire and attached to the hooks that remained in the wall.

Remove plug in air fresheners or motion activated air fresheners, so that they do not interfere with any smells brought by spirit.

Whatever equipment you intend to use in your circle, should be introduced into the circle from the first sitting regardless of whether you intend to use it from the first week. Everything is energy and if you introduce say a spirit trumpet three months into sitting, again the dynamics will be changed and spirit have to make adjustments; it is time consuming.

It is a myth that all newly formed circles should start off sitting in total black out conditions. It is true that phenomena can generally be achieved far quicker in the darkened conditions, however, it offers no evidential value, and your circle could at some point in time be open to allegations of fraud. I highly recommend that from the first sitting that some form of lighting is used; it is far better for the circle guides to be given the sitting conditions of your choice from the beginning, rather than phenomena occurring and you having a desire for light to be introduced, so that you can actually witness the proceedings some months or even years down the road of development. By introducing light after development has started will simply halt the development and generally the circle guides have to start from the beginning again. Yes it may well take longer to see results, but well worth the wait!

A lamp, with a low wattage bulb, preferably on a dimmer switch that the guides can alter for themselves. White, red, blue or green bulbs or candle light are all good forms of lighting.

Choosing Suitable Sitters

Intention plays a big part in circle development and 'like attracts like' is very relevant when choosing the right sitters for the circle. Not everyone is a suitable sitter. A person who has a huge ego and wants to put their own development before the group as a whole would be unsuitable. Newly bereaved are also unsuitable. Bereavement is a time in our lives when we are very needy, regardless of our belief system. When we lose someone whom we love, it is natural to have a longing to see that person again, even if its just one last time, therefore the bereaved may well state and believe that they are not focusing on only their loved one coming through in circle, but alas it would not be true. The other sitters also have a natural desire to focus on the bereaved person's loved one in order to assist with the healing process. The mindset of sitters has to be of an open heart to welcome any communicator that wishes to step forward and when focus is only on one person, the development of the group is held back.

When a circle is established and a sitter suffers bereavement, it is advisable for the sitter to take a break from the circle until they have had sufficient time to heal and mourn their loss.
Some of you reading this book may find my words harsh or believe me to be unsympathetic; I most certainly don't wish to come across as either. The circle once developed will hopefully bring much comfort and support to the bereaved through your work with spirit, but that is the end product not the developmental stage. Like everything you have a choice and I can only impart to you all I have learnt, it is up to each of you, when faced with this situation, to decide what action is best taken.

I have advised many circles, both here in the United Kingdom and abroad, on circle development. One of the most recurring problems that sitters or circle leaders write to me about is sitters having been chosen to sit based on pure friendship and not their suitability. It is a difficult thing to say 'no' to a friend when they ask to be part of a newly formed circle, especially when you know they are not suitable. However, unfortunately for the sake of the development and the sitters that will be giving their time and energy each week you have a responsibility not to feel obliged to say 'yes'. A true friend will understand.

I would advise against having sitters with mental health issues are addicted to recreational drugs or are alcohol dependent.

A successful circle has five key ingredients:

a)   Harmony
b)   Dedication
c)   Patience
d)   Trust
e)   Intentions

Look at each of your chosen sitters; assess them individually on each of these key elements. Does each of your sitters enjoy each other's company? Is there are friction between any of them?

Getting the right sitters to travel this journey with you is crucial, so it is worth taking your time in choosing them. Remember you can have a physical medium with the most outstanding ability but without the right sitters, development will fail.

Identifying the physical medium and choosing the circle leader

Most mediums that have physical mediumship abilities would have experienced phenomena around them, generally from childhood. Most adults would confuse this with poltergeist activity. When this is the case, then the task of the circle leader, once good sitters have been chosen, is all that remains to be established. The circle leader ideally will have some knowledge of physical mediumship, but it is not essential. The circle leader needs to be a good communicator who will be responsible for circle procedures and who can be strong but calm should any situation arise during the circle sitting. Most circles form without an identified physical medium and await some communication from spirit to indicate whether the production of phenomena will be possible, or in the absence of a physical medium in the circle, should sit for development in a different area of mediumship. Some circles with the right blends of energy from the sitters are well suited for phenomena using strictly energy only. Therefore the presence of a physical medium is not necessarily needed. However, I am not aware of any energy-based circle ever having produced evidence of survival, but the phenomena can be quite extraordinary.

Sitting Procedure

It is important to remember that when you sit for development in the circle, that it is very much a joint effort on both sides of the vibrations. As we make appointments on the physical plane say to visit the dentist or doctor, so we make an appointment with our spirit guides in the circle. It is crucial therefore that a suitable day and time for sitting each week is agreed amongst all the sitters and that everyone arrives promptly. It should be the same day and time each week thereafter.

Music should be played in the room where the sitting will be taking place for 30 minutes before the sitting; it helps to lift the vibrations in the room.

Once everyone has arrived for the sitting each should choose a seat in the circle. This seat should then become that sitters permanent seat each sitting. If there is a medium that has been identified, then he or she should take the seat in the cabinet.

The circle leader should open in prayer and close the circle in prayer.

A few songs should be sung to raise the vibrations further. The sitting should last for about one hour and you should be disciplined with your sitting lengths. Working on a physical level with spirit is initially very draining. Sitters often have feelings of nausea or pain in or around the solar plexus, and they can suffer with headaches or dizziness. It is important for the sittings to remain fairly short so that the sitters can become accustomed to sitting using physical energy. Water should be drunk before and after the sitting by all attendees. As each sitting passes, the physical effects will be felt less and less and the sitters will then begin to feel energized and uplifted after each sitting.

Conversations during the sitting should be of an uplifting nature. No bad news or painful experiences should be brought into the conversation, no foul language, remember 'like attracts like' as you wish to connect to only those of the purest intentions from spirit side.

No alcohol or recreational drugs should be consumed or used on the day of the sitting. Food should be consumed at least two hours before the sitting; this will help to alleviate some of the physical discomforts associated with working on a physical level.

Keys and loose change should be left outside the circle, and no lighters or torches should be brought into the room where the sitting is to be held.

During the sitting refrain from clapping, it disperses the energy you have built.

Do not whistle or whisper; one of the first signs of direct voice being achieved is whistling or whispering and you need to acknowledge these sounds if you hear them.

Intentions and aspirations should be spoken about openly in circle. Guides, although they may not be able to communicate with you initially, will be able to hear you. They will want to know what you hope the eventual outcome for the circle will be. If you are hoping for the circle to be used to produce direct voice for instance, tell them. It may not be possible with the energies in circle but they will always experiment and if possible work towards your goal.

Don't forget laughter, lots of laughter, it is excellent for achieving harmony amongst the sitters and raising the vibrations in the room, and of course spirit have a sense of humor too!

Remain vigilant throughout the sitting. If you see or hear something or even think you have, acknowledge it verbally. This draws the other sitters attention to it, but also, spirit don't know if they are actually being received by you. In the case of direct voice, spirit project their thoughts to form words in our vibration so that we can hear them and hold conversations with them; however, they can hear us respond but they are unable to hear their own voices, so need to be acknowledged that they can indeed be heard.

What phenomena can be achieved when a physical medium is present in circle?

Spirit lights
Spirit mists and orbs
EVP
Levitation of objects and people
Elongation
Apports
Transfiguration
Spirit Photography
Direct voice (through a spirit trumpet)
Independent direct voice (from a space in mid air)
Direct writing (spirit manifest a hand and picks up pen and writes)
Materialization

Some of the above phenomena can be achieved without the presence of a physical medium, such as EVP, spirit lights, mists and orbs.

Not every physical medium will have the ability to be used to produce all of the above phenomena.

Trance

Trance is not a favourable form of communication with me personally. It can be useful to make connections with the guides and to assist in any instructions that the guides may have for the circle by way of assisting with the development. However, I am a strong believer that trance communication can and often does interfere with the communication from guides, as the mediums mind will always play an active part.

Trance alone is not physical mediumship, but is often used in physical circles.

Trance is used on two levels, the conscious and the unconscious level. Often ectoplasmic mediums are entranced to an unconscious level, when ectoplasm is being withdrawn from them. It is a necessary process for some, for the safety of the medium. When the medium has developed sufficiently, the guides may no longer have a need to entrance the medium.

One final thing, never touch anything that has been produced by spirit unless given permission to do so by the circle guides. Ectoplasm burns and if touched without permission can retract into the mediums body with force.

Most of all enjoy sitting with each other and for the love of spirit, and your circle will flourish.

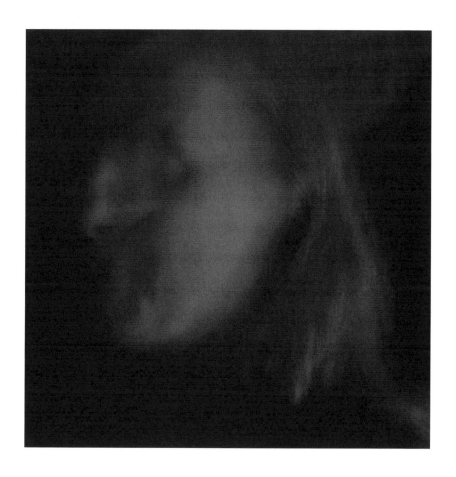

Meditations

Meditation is the key to developing your spiritual gifts, but it also brings other benefits too, such as inner peace and calmness. It helps to elevate stress and nervous complaints, and can create a space for oneness, a place where we can be free from the physical world and all our emotions that can weigh us down.

Here are the meditations that I used, but you can adapt them as you wish, to suit your own needs.

Daily meditation - Easy level

Close your eyes and relax in a peaceful place where you will not get disturbed. Say a prayer. Still your mind and listen to your breath. Imagine you have a trap door above your head. Throw open your trap door and allow the universal energy to rush towards you and down through your trap door, allow it to fill every part of your physical body and extend into your auric field. It is a beautiful golden light. Continue to relax and listening to your breath. This universal energy brings you love and fulfillment, feel its warmth and its love. Sit in its power for as long as you can each day. Close your trap door, and say a prayer filled with love and thanks.

To free yourself of materialism

Relax, say a prayer, open your trap doors and fill yourself with the universal energy. Keep listening to your breath and as you relax, find yourself sitting on the edge of a forest, a beautiful enchanting forest. See yourself living joyfully in the forest. Know it has everything you need to live free from desire. Water, food and shelter and in harmony with all nature that lives beside you. Give thanks to all that the universe brings to us. Close your trap door and go about your day fulfilled with nourishment from the forest.

Cleansing

Relax, say a prayer and listen to your breath. Open your trap door and fill yourself with the universal energy. Keep listening to your breath and as you relax find yourself sitting on a boulder beneath a beautiful waterfall with crystal clear water streaked with silver and gold. It glistens in the sunlight. Allow the waterfall to completely wash over you, cleansing your physical body and auric field. All negativity is washed away and you feel refreshed and full of vitality, you have clarity of mind. Give thanks for its cleansing power. Close your trap door.

Discover your spiritual pathway

Relax, say a prayer and listen to your breath. Open your trap door and fill yourself with the universal energy. As you continue to listen to your breath, find yourself sitting on a large rock on a beautiful beach, filled with golden sand and a crystal blue sea. Hear the waves crashing against your rock, feel the sea breeze blowing through your hair, smell the salt from the sea and hear the gulls overhead. Feel yourself connected to the universe. Stare into the distance of the ocean; ask for your spiritual pathway to be shown to you. Start to see on the horizon your pathway coming towards you, as it moves closer towards you clarity of vision comes to you. Do not worry if you do not see it clearly; keep repeating this meditation until you do see it, in all its glory. Give thanks to those that guide you. Close your trap door.

Transformation

Relax, say a prayer and listen to your breath. Open your
trap door and fill yourself with the universal energy. As
you continue to listen to your breath, you become aware
of being cocooned in a protective shell. You can see out
but nothing can penetrate it or see into it. Focus on what
you desire to be transformed, it could be to have a well
physical body, clarity of purpose or to be free from
financial constraints, whatever transformation you desire.
See and feel the changes that are taking place within your
cocoon, without interference from outside influences.
Keep listening to your breath and know the
transformation is taking place. Reaffirm it in your mind.
As the transformation takes place the cocoon starts to
crack like an egg, keep focusing on the transformation
that is taking place, as the cocoon breaks away, come
forth from the cocoon transformed like the butterfly. Give
thanks. Some transformations take a period of time to be
fully achieved, so repeat daily until the full
transformation has been reached. Close your trap door.

Meet your spirit guide

Relax and say a prayer, listen to your breath. Open your
trap door and fill yourself with the universal energy. As
you continue to listen to your breath, you find yourself
sitting on a stone bench, in the most beautiful garden. It
is filled with brightly colored flowers with the most
wonderful aromas, you can hear birds singing and feel the
breeze gently blowing through your hair. Butterflies are
gently fluttering around you and the trees are laden with
blossom. As you look into the meadows that extend
beyond your garden, you can see a ball of golden light; it
is shimmering with gold and silver streaks. The ball of

light radiates love and warmth to you and it brings a feeling of peace and calmness. This ball of light slowly starts to move closer to you, you get a sense of the energy, male, female, and the wisdom they bring to you. You communicate through telepathy and the responses will come. Ask whatever you wish; ask this energy to reveal themselves to you, in all their glory as there true self. Thank them for coming and re-affirm your intention and desire to go forth on your spiritual journey. Close your trap door. Repeat this daily until your guide has fully revealed him/herself to you.

Last words

I hope you have enjoyed having access to 'my world', the life of a physical medium. It has been a lonely and difficult path that I have walked at times, but it has truly brought me great joy, knowledge and inspiration.

My work continues on a scientific level, with further Skype experiments being carried out, and evidence that is being recorded for future reference. My circle continues to sit and the developments progress at a steady pace, always focusing on survival evidence for the purpose of healing and advancements for science.

I continue to teach workshops and courses, which brings me personal fulfillment. Knowledge is always to be gained and shared for future physical mediums that walk the same pathway.

My healing continues to evolve too. With new techniques being developed by my wonderful loving guides that means a far greater amount of people will eventually benefit from their energies, no matter where they are in the world.

I know some that have taken the time to read this book, will be at the beginning of their spiritual journeys, and I wish you well in all your discoveries of the ways of spirit; it is an exciting road you walk.

For now, I leave you with these parting words ....

"All according to plan "...
(Red Cloud)

If you wish to contact me please feel free to e mail me at:
jo.bradleycircle@talktalk.net

Printed in Great Britain
by Amazon